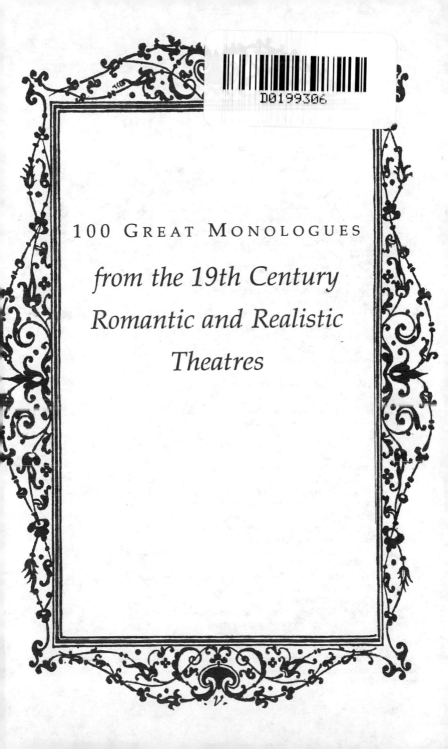

100 GREAT MONOLOGUES

from the 19th Century
Romantic and Realistic
Theatres

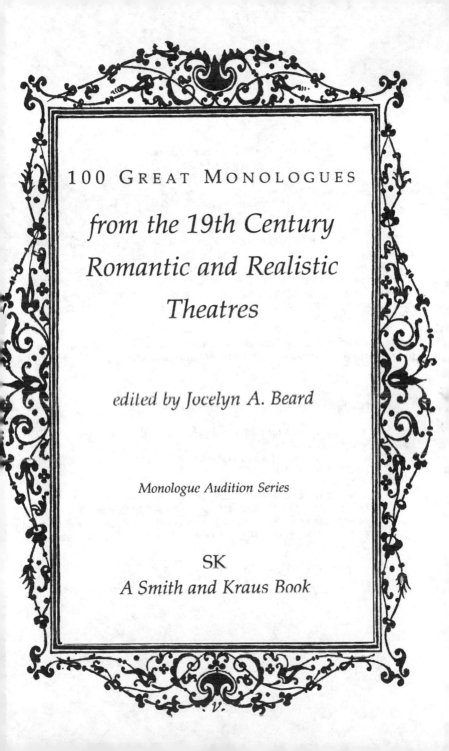

100 GREAT MONOLOGUES

from the 19th Century Romantic and Realistic Theatres

edited by Jocelyn A. Beard

Monologue Audition Series

SK
A Smith and Kraus Book

v.

Published by Smith and Kraus, Inc.
One Main Street, Lyme, NH 03768

First Edition: November 1994
9 8 7 6 5 4 3 2 1

NOTE: These monologues are intended to be used for audition and class study; permission is not required to use the material for those purposes.

Library of Congress Cataloging-in-Publication Data

100 Great monologues from the 19th century romantic and realistic theatres / edited by Jocelyn Beard. --1st ed.
        p. cm. --(Monologue audition series)
    ISBN 1-880399-61-X : $9.95

    1. Monologues. 2. Acting--Auditions. 3. European drama--19th centu ry--translations into English. 4. English drama--19th century. 5. American drama--19th century. I. Beard, Jocelyn. II. Title: One hundred great monologues from the 19th century romantic and realistic theatres. III. Series.

PN2080.A123   1994
808.82'45--dc20
                             94-33110
                             CIP

This is for Milette,
Best Friend and Miracle Worker,
with love.

—*Jocelyn A. Beard*

Contents

MEN'S MONOLOGUES

Foreword

Imagine: you and a partner whirl around the ballroom floor in time with a stirring Viennese waltz. Candles flicker from every chandelier illuminating all the dancing couples in endless succession in the floor-to-ceiling mirrors that line the room. In a smaller salon women tell each others' fortunes with tarot cards while whispering the tale of poor Marie, who committed suicide when the man she loved married another. Suddenly, a savage cry rings out, silencing the orchestra. The couples glide to a stand-still, all eyes fixed on the balcony door. It is Marie! (The rumor of her death was greatly exaggerated.) In her trembling hand is a small pistol which is aimed at the very heart of Georges, the man who so cruelly spurned her. By the wall a dowager faints and young gentlemen rush to wave smelling salts beneath her nose. Georges' fiancee screams and throws herself in front of the man she loves. A shot rings out and...

Welcome to Volume Three: Romanticism. In Volume Two of this series we saw the rise of Neo-Classicism and the desire for the order and beauty of the classical world. Something this perfect could only last so long, I mean, we're only human, for Pete's sake! I don't want to live the righteous and fatal life of Antigone any more than I want to watch someone else doing it for very long. Fortunately, most people agree, and so the turbulent end of the 18th century gave rise to the birth of Romanticism.

Intellect and reason are out, imagination and emotions are in! The French Revolution forever changed the tone of society in Europe, and with it the tone of theatre. Idealistic new voices began to emerge throughout the Continent, all sharing the Romantic obsession with the morbid and the melancholy. Great poets like Keats, Byron and Shelley all created dark works of dire emotion for the stage, creating worlds full of supernatural agents and doomed fates. Gothic dramas like De Monfort introduce us to men driven to madness by feelings of jealousy and rage. For a breath of fresh air, turn to writers like Kleist, who concentrated on the lighter side of the movement while reveling in the absurd nature of life as can be seen in his masterpiece, *The Broken Jug*. The pinnacle of the movement in theatre, in my opinion, is *Danton's Death*, by Buchner. Here is the accumulated fury of a revolution and of the people whose lives it destroyed and saved; the very heart of the Romantic Movement.

This was a time of empire and expansion, and as the world grew smaller and smaller, the time of the romantics slowly came to an end. But there, suddenly, was our own beloved modern theatre in all of its Ibsen/Shaw/Chekhov/Wilde glory.

I leave you now, with the world teetering on the brink of its first round of global madness: WWI. Close your eyes, listen for the waltz and be swept away.

Break A Leg!

Jocelyn A. Beard
Summer 1994
Patterson, New York

100 GREAT MONOLOGUES

from the 19th Century
Romantic and Realistic
Theatres

Women's Monologues

Amphitryon

Heinrich Von Kleist, tr. by Martin Greenberg
1807

Scene: The Palace of Amphitryon in Thebes

Dramatic

> Alcmene: wife of Amphitryon, Commander-in-Chief of the Thebians. A woman
> deceived by Zeus, 20s

Alcmene has been tricked by Zeus into thinking that the lusty god is, in fact, her
husband. The lord of Olympus has prepared a series of misadventures for the
real Amphitryon that will keep him away from the palace while he seduces Alcmene. When the real Amphitryon finally returns to his home, Alcmene no
longer recognizes him, and here demands that he leave.

ALCMENE: Vile creature! Odious man!
You dare to call me so? Before my husband's
awe-commanding countenance, I am
not shielded from your mania? You monster!
Far more hideous to me than bloated
shapes that squat in fens! What harm did I
do you that you should creep up on me under
cover of a night engendered out of Hell
and dribble your disgusting venom on my wings?
What more than that I caught your eye, corrupted
creature, like a glowworm, in the silence?
Oh, finally it's clear to me the mad
delusion under which I labored. What I
needed was the brightness of the sun by which to see
the difference between the cringing figure
of a vulgar peasant and the heroic architecture
of these royal limbs, between the ox and stag.
A curse on senses that surrendered to so gross
a hoax, a breast that rang so falsely to the touch,
a soul so little worth as not to know
its own true love! Without a sentry to mount guard
on my heart and keep it blameless,
I'll hide myself away, I swear,
where nothing lives, on a mountain peak not even

visited by owls. Your odious
deceit's succeeded, go! My peace of soul
is snapped and broken now.

The Bankrupt

George Henry Boker
1853

Scene: London

#1—Dramatic

Amy: a woman whose marriage is on the brink of ruin, 20–30

Amy's husband, Edward, has run afoul of a plot to ruin him financially. His
enemy's final coup is to trick Edward into thinking that Amy has been unfaithful.
When Edward angrily demands that Amy leave their house, she tearfully begs
him to allow her to stay, if only to be a mother to their children.

AMY: Edward, I beseech you to pardon me! I do not ask to be your
wife again; I only beg to be allowed to remain near you—wait upon
you—to toil for you—to be your slave. Lest you should think my hu-
mility beneath me, it is not for your sake, alone, I ask it. A mother's
heart cries through my lowly prayer. What will our young and helpless children do when I am far away? Whose hand shall smooth their
pillows; or allay our little sufferers' agonies when sickness withers
them? Whose hand shall join their rosy palms in prayer to the great
power whom we so much offend? And if Heaven's wisdom should
remove them hence, as it has done with one before their time—the
child we buried in the spring, my husband, among the violets and
early flowers, dropped like a severed bud—oh! then, what hand
would not desecrate the dead, if it performed those offices of love
which Heaven has sanctified to me alone? Think of it well. I only ask
to live beside my children. I promise you, I will not vex your
thoughts, by keeping my poor person in your sight!
[*GILT:* Your female eloquence is lost on me. I prepared myself for
these tricks of the tongue.]
AMY: Edward, you are not yourself. I know that trade has hardened
you, day by day, and that the absorbing lust of gain has slowly
usurped the place in your heart which belongs to your family by
right; but I never thought that you would so far forget your better nature, as to resist a plea such as this, even from the lips of a stranger. I
am not weeping to make you pity me. I do not wish to soften you by
any but rational means. These tears are shed over the disgrace which
is about to fall upon our children. You have no right to forget them in

your passion. You have no right—Oh! Edward, if my heart breaks down, and I am so choked with sorrow, my silence does not prove my cause unjust. (*Weeps.*)

#2—Dramatic
Amy

Believing her to have been unfaithful, Edward demands that Amy leave and take the children with her, for after all, he has no reason to suspect that they are his. This is the final insult to virtuous Amy, whose patience is finally at an end.

AMY: Ruffian! You have insulted me, and cast stain upon your guilt-less children! Here, the pride of my poor, trampled sex can rise sub-lime against you! Till you spoke those words, the gates of love were open wide between us; now they have closed, forever, with a clash that startled those above us. Heaven grant, that its pity stopped the ears of our departed child against its father's voice, so that its saintly joy may not be marred! I will not ask you, sir, to seek our Nelly's grave, and keep it clear of weeds. No, no! the weeds, and noxious things, would sprout beneath your eyes. I will do all that duty, and such love as never entered in your callous heart, can do for Nelly's memory. Never, if you have any sense of shame, never dare meet me by that little grave!
[*GILT:* Amy!—]
AMY: Peace! I bore the foulest and most unjust taunts man ever heaped on woman, calmly, from your lips—I bore your brutal man-ner, when you cast me from you almost with a blow; but, now, you dare despise your offspring, soil the glittering links that Heaven let down to us—and in Heaven's name, and with Heaven's dread au-thority, I say to you that you, Edward Giltwood, have committed sac-rilege! I, who have neither power nor will to just you here, shall see you judged before all-powerful Heaven! Farewell! May some good spirit come to you, and bend your stubborn heart to better ways! My influence over you is gone forever. Look!—look in my eyes—and see my innocence! Look!—for you've taken your last gaze on me! (*Exit.*)

Bertram or
The Castle of St. Aldobrand
Charles Robert Maturin
1816

Scene: England

Dramatic
Imogene: a woman teetering on the brink of madness, 30s

Believing her beloved Bertram to be dead, Imogene marries a man she doesn't love to save her father from ruin. When Bertram returns and discovers her marriage, he kills her husband in a jealous rage. Imogene takes her young son and flees to a monastery. Here, she is haunted by the grisly spectre of her husband's corpse.

IMOGENE (*Looking round on the chapel, after a long pause.*):
They've left me—all things leave me—all things human—
Follower and friend—last went the man of God—
The last—but yet he went—
[*CHILD:* —I will not leave thee—]
IMOGENE: My son, my son, was that thy voice—
When heaven and angels, earth and earthly things
Do leave the guilty in their guiltiness—
A cherub's voice doth whisper in a child's.
"There is a shrine within thy little heart
"Where I will hide, nor hear the trump of doom—"
[*CHILD:* Dear mother, take me home—]
Imogene: Thou hast no home—
She, whom thou callest mother left thee none.
We're hunted from mankind—(*Sinking down.*)
"Here will we lie in darkness down together,
"And sleep in a dreamless sleep—what form is that—"
Why have they laid him there? (*Recoiling.*)
Plain in the gloomy depth he lies before me
The cold blue wound whence blood hath ceased to flow;
The stormy[1] clenching of the bared teeth—
The gory socket that the balls have burst from—

[1] The Larpent version has "stoney."

I see them all— (*Shrieking.*)
It moves—it moves—it rises—it comes on me—
'Twill break th' eternal silence of the grave—
'Twill wind me in its creaking marrowless arms.
Hold up thy hands to it, it was thy father—
Ah, it would have thee too, off—save me—off—
(*Rushes out with the child.*)

Bianca Visconti or
The Heart Overtasked

Nathaniel Parker Willis
1830

Scene: 14th century Milan

#1—Dramatic
   Bianca: heiress to the throne of Milan, 18–20

   Bianca's father, the Duke of Milan, has just decreed that she will marry Sforza, a
   young nobleman with whom she has always been in love. Here, she shares the
   happy news with her servants.

BIANCA: To marry Sforza!
My dream come true! my long, long cherished dream!
The star come out of heaven that I had worshipped!
The paradise I built with soaring fancy
And filled with rapture like a honey-bee
Dropped from the clouds at last! Am I awake?—
Am I awake, dear Giulio?
[*PAGE* (*Half advancing to her.*): Noble mistress!]
BIANCA: Thank God, they speak to me! It is no dream!
It was *this* hand my father took to tell me—
It was with *these* lips that I tried to speak—
It was *this* heart that beat its giddy prison
As if exulting joy new-sprung within it
Would out and fill the world! . . . .
. . . . Wed him tomorrow!
So suddenly a wife! Will it seem modest,
With but twelve hours of giddy preparation
To come a bride to church! Will he remember
I was ten years ago affianced to him?
I have had time to think on't! Oh, I'll tell him—
When I dare speak, I'll tell him—how I've loved him!
And day and night dreamed of him, and through all
The changing wars treasured the solemn troth
Broke by my father! If he listens kindly,
I'll tell him how I fed my eyes upon him

In Venice at his triumph—when he walked
Like a descended god beside the Doge,
Who thanked him for his victories, and the people,
From every roof and balcony, by thousands
Shouted out "Sforza! Live the gallant Sforza!"
I was a child then—but I felt my heart
Grow, in one hour, to woman!

#2—Dramatic
        Bianca

> Following her wedding to Sforza, Bianca discovers that her childish dreams of
> life together won't be enough to hold the interest of a man intent on glory. Here,
> she vows to win his love in earnest, even if it means the death of her heart's de-
> sire.

BIANCA: He does not love me!
I never dreamed of this! To be his bride
Was all the heaven I looked for! Not to love me
When I have been ten years affianced to him!—
When I have lived for him—shut up my heart,
With every pulse and hope, for his use only—
Worshipped—oh, God! idolatrously loved him!
. . . .
Why has he sought to marry me? Why still
Renew the broken pledge my father made him?
Why, for ten years, with war and policy,
Strive for my poor alliance? . . . .
. . . . He *must* love me,
Or I shall break my heart! I never had
One other hope in life! I never linked
One thought, but to this chain! I have no blood—
No breath—no being—separate from Sforza!
Nothing has any other name! The sun
Shined like his smile—the lightning was his glory—
The night his sleep, and the hushed moon watched o'er him;—
Stars writ his name—his breath hung on the flowers—
Music had no voice but to say *I love him*,
And life no future, but his love for me!

Whom does he love? Marancio's wife? He praised
Only her courage! Queen Giovanna's beauty?
'Tis dust these many years! There is no sign
He loves another, and report said ever
His *glory* was his mistress. *Can* he love?
Shame on the doubt! 'Twas written in the ring
"He who loves *most*, loves honor best"—and Sforza
Is made too like a god to lack a heart.
And do, I breathe again! To make him love me
Is all my life now! to pry through his nature,
And find his heart out. That's wrapt in his glory!
I'll feed his glory, then! He praised Giovanna
That she was royal and magnificent—
Ay—that's well thought on, too! How should an eye,
Dazzled with war and warlike pomp, like Sforza's,
Find pleasure in simplicity like mine! (*Looks at her dress.*)
I'm a duke's daughter, and I'll wear the look on't.
Unlock my jewels and my costly robes,
And while I keep his show-struck eye upon me,
Watch for a golden opportunity
To build up his renown! . . . .
. . . . And so farewell
The gentle world I've lived in! Farewell all
My visions of a world for two hearts only—
Sforza's and mine! If I outlive this change,
So brief and yet so violent within me,
I'll come back in my dreams, oh, childish world!
If not—a broken heart blots out remembrance. (*Exit into her bridal chamber, which is seen beyond on opening the door.*)

The Broken Jug

Heinrich von Kleist, tr. by Martin Greenberg
1808

Scene: a Flemish village

Serio-comic
> Frau Martha: a woman seeking retribution in a court of law, 40–50

> In the midst of a domestic altercation, Frau Martha's prized jug is smashed. Determined to be compensated for her loss, she brings the matter before the local magistrate. Here, she describes the jug to the court.

FRAU MARTHA: You see it, do you, worthy sirs, this jug?
[*ADAM:* We do.]
FRAU MARTHA: You don't—begging your pardon.
You see pieces—the loveliest jug that ever
was now lies in pieces. Right where this hole
is, all the Netherlands were handed over
to the Spanish Philip. Here Emperor Charles
stood in his royal robes. Those are his legs,
that's all that's left of him. Here Philip knelt
before his father to receive the crown—he's
still there, down to his backside,
but even it did not get off without a whack.
There his two aunts, the Queens of France and Hungary,
so touched, are dabbing at their eyes with handkerchiefs—
but now one of them looks like she is weeping
for herself. Here's Sir Philibert in the retinue,
still leaning on his sword, spared destruction
by the Emperor's catching it—but he'll
fall on his face now, him and that damned Maximilian,
because they haven't any swords to lean on.
Here at the center with his miter on
once stood the Archbishop of Arras—the devil
came and carried him away. All
that's left of him is his long shadow on the pavement.
In the background, standing in a circle in close
order, were the Royal Guards with halberds

and spears. And just look here and you can see
the houses lining the great marketplace of Brussels,
and from a window someone peering curiously.
But what there is for him to see now, I don't know.
[ADAM: Frau Martha! They broke the treaty,[2] yes, but spare
us that. The hole your jug got, that's our business
here, and not the provinces surrendered on it.]
FRAU MARTHA: I beg to differ, Judge! The beauty of the jug
is our business!—Childeric the tinker
captured it when the Prince of Orange and his fighting
tars took Briel. A Spaniard was about to put
it to his lips and drink it dry when Childeric
came up on him from behind and cut him down
and drank up all the wine himself and went his way.
[*ADAM:* A true Dutchman, that one was!]
FRAU MARTHA: Fürchtegott[3]
the gravedigger inherited it next. A sobersided
man, no rioter: three times he drank
from it, all told, and even so he mixed
his wine with water. The first time was,
when he reached sixty and married a young thing;
three years later, when she rejoiced
his heart by presenting him with an heir; and after
she had borne him fifteen children, he drank
from it a third time, when she died.
[*ADAM:* Oh, that's good, that's good!]
FRAU MARTHA: The next hands
it came into were Zacharias',
a tailor out of Tirlemont, who told
my husband, him of blessed memory,
with his own mouth, what I'm about to tell
to you. When the Frenchmen came a-plundering
he pitched the jug and with it everything
he owned straight out the window, then jumped out of it

[2] The Treaty of Brussels, 1555, whose inauguration is depicted on the jug.
[3] *Fürchtegott:* "Fear God."

himself and broke his neck, the oaf, but the jug,
an earthenware one, made of clay, it landed
on its feet and never broke.

[*ADAM:* Get to the point, Frau Martha Rull, the point!]

FRAU MARTHA: Then in sixty-six, in the great fire, by
which time it had come into the possession of my husband, bless
his soul—

[*ADAM:* The devil, woman, is there any end in sight?]

FRAU MARTHA: If I am not to speak, Judge Adam,
I see no purpose in my coming here.
I'll say good-bye and find a court where I
am listened to.

The Bucktails or Americans in England

James Kirke Paulding
1847

Scene: Bath, England

Dramatic

Jane Warfield: an American heiress, 20

While visiting her sister in London, Jane is kidnapped by a gang of ruffians who intend to hold her for ransom. Fortunately, Jane manages to escape, and here seeks refuge in a churchyard.

JANE: Behold! A Christian temple!—
Hail, dear asylum, I will rest me here,
Within the peaceful precincts of the dead!
If guilt and crime, hypocrisy and fraud,
In shrines like this from their just punishment
Have oft found refuge, I can't seek in vain,
That flee not from my own, but other's wrongs.
(*Seats herself in the porch.*)
How solemn is the night! I, I alone
Here breathe among the dead of ages past!
See! where the stones point to the dust below,
And tell a tale of flattery, that would make
The bloodless corses blush if they could hear it.
Why should I tremble? "Dead men tell no tales,"
And such a scene seems fit for deeds of guilt
That never should be told!
But dead men do no harm, and ev'n the wretch
Whose harden'd soul ne'er shrunk before His eye,
Who sees all that is done, or will'd, or thought,
Quails at the glaring of the sightless corse,
And stands corrected by its mute cold lips,
That tell what all must come to.
I'll rest me here till morning.

Cain

Lord Byron
1815

Scene: the land without paradise

Dramatic
> Eve: mother of Cain and Abel

Upon discovering the fact that Cain has murdered Abel, Eve curses her surviving son and banishes him from her sight.

EVE: Hear, Jehovah!
May the eternal serpent's curse be on him!
For he was fitter for his seed than ours.
May all his days be desolate! May—
[*ADAM:* Hold!
Curse him not, mother, for he is thy son—
Curse him not, mother, for he is my brother,
And my betroth'd.]
EVE: He hath left thee no brother—
Zillah no husband—me *no son!*—for thus
I curse him from my sight for evermore!
All bonds I break between us, as he broke
That of his nature, in yon—Oh death! death!
Why didst thou not take me, who first incurr'd thee?
Why dost thou not so now?
[*ADAM:* Eve! let not this,
Thy natural grief, lead to impiety!
A heavy doom was long forespoken to us;
And now that it begins, let it be borne
In such sort as may show our God that we
Are faithful servants to his holy will.]
EVE (*Pointing to Cain.*): *His will!* the will of you incarnate spirit
Of death, whom I have brought upon the earth
To strew it with the dead. May all the curses
Of life be on him! and his agonies
Drive him forth o'er the wilderness, like us
From Eden, till his children do by him

As he did by his brother! May the swords
And wings of fiery cherubim pursue him
By day and night—snakes spring up in his path—
Earth's fruits be ashes in his mouth—the leaves
On which he lays his head to sleep be strew'd
With scorpions! May his dreams be of his victim!
His waking a continual dread of death!
May the clear rivers turn to blood as he
Stoops down to stain them with his raging lip!
May every element shun or change to him!
May he live in the pangs which other die with!
And death itself wax something worse than death
To him who first acquainted him with man!
Hence, fratricide! henceforth that word is *Cain*,
Through all the coming myriads of mankind,
Who shall abhor thee though thou wert their sire!
May the grass wither from thy feet! the woods
Deny thee shelter! earth a home! the dust
A grave! the sun his light! and heaven her God!

The Captive

Matthew G. Lewis
1803

Scene: a dungeon

Dramatic

      The Captive: a woman held prisoner, 20s

    Accused of madness, this desperate woman struggles with futile abandon against the chains that imprison her in Bedlam.

(The scene represents a dungeon, in which is a grated door, guarded by strong bars and chains. In the upper part is an open gallery, leading to the cells above. Slow and melancholy music. The Captive is discovered in the attitude of hopeless grief:—she is in chains;—her eyes are fixed, with a vacant stare, and her hands are folded.

    After a pause, the Gaoler is seen passing through the upper gallery with a lamp: he appears at the grate, and opens the door. The noise of the bars falling rouses the Captive. She looks round eagerly; but on seeing the Gaoler enter, she waves her hand mournfully, and relapses into her former stupor. The Gaoler replenishes the jug with water, and places a loaf of bread by her side. He then prepares to leave the dungeon, when the Captive seems to resolve on making an attempt to excite his compassion: she rises from her bed of straw, clasps his hand, and sinks at his feet. The music ceases, and she speaks.)

THE CAPTIVE:

Stay, Gaoler, stay, and hear my woe!

    She is not mad who kneels to thee,

For what I'm now too well I know,

    And what I was, and what should be.

I'll rave no more in proud despair;

    My language shall be mild,[4] though sad:

But yet I'll firmly, truly swear,

    I am not mad! *(Then kissing his hand.)* I am not mad!

(He offers to leave her; she detains him, and continues, in a tone of eager persuasion.)

---

[4]The Larpent and *Memoirs* versions have "calm."

My tyrant husband forged the tale,

　　Which chains me in this dreary cell:[5]

My fate unknown my Friends bewail—

　　Oh! Gaoler, haste that fate to tell!

Oh! haste my Father's heart to tell!

　　His heart at once 'twill grieve and glad

To know, though kept a Captive here,

　　I am not mad! I am not mad![6]

(Harsh music, while the Gaoler, with a look of contempt and disbelief, forces his hand from her grasp, and leaves her. The bars are heard replacing.)

He smiles in scorn, and turns the key![7]

　　He quits the grate! I knelt in vain!—

His glimmering Lamp still... still I see! 　[8]

(Music expressing the light growing fainter,[9] as the Gaoler retires through the gallery, and the Captive watches his departure with eager looks.)

　　'Tis gone[10] . . . and all is gloom again!

(She shivers, and wraps her garment more closely around her.)

Cold, bitter cold!—no warmth!—no light!

　　Life, all thy comforts once I had;

Yet here I'm chain'd this freezing night,

　　(Eagerly.) Although not mad! No, [no, no,] no! not mad!

(A few bars of melancholy music, which she interrupts, by exclaiming suddenly.)

'Tis sure some dream! some vision vain!—

　　(Proudly.) What? I, the child of rank and wealth,

Am I the wretch who clanks this chain,

　　Bereft of freedom, friends and health?

Ah! While I dwell on blessings fled,

---

[5]The Larpent version has "A tyrant husband forged the tale/And chained me in this dreary Cell."

[6]The Larpent and *Memoirs* versions have "I am not mad! not mad! not mad!"

[7]The Larpent and *Memoirs* versions have "He turns the key!"

[8]The Larpent and *Memoirs* versions have "Still—still, his glimmering lamp I see."

[9]This stage direction gives us some idea of the demands made upon the composers for both monodramas and melodramas, in this case upon Dr. Thomas Busby (1755–1838) whose efforts for Lewis's play were praised by the *Monthly Mirror* of 15 April 1803: "Dr. Busby's music was admirably adapted to the action and character of the subject, and displayed great depth of science, and knowledge of effect."

[10]The Larpent and *Memoirs* versions have "'Tis lost!"

Which never more my heart must glad,
How aches my heart! how burns my head!—[11]
(*Interrupting herself hastily, and pressing her hands forcibly against her forehead.*)

But 'tis not mad!—no! 'Tis not mad!
(*She remains fixed in this attitude, with a look of fear, till the music, changing, expresses that some tender, melancholy reflection has passed her mind.*)

[My child!—My child!]
Hast thou, my Child, forgot ere this[12]
A mother's face, a mother's tongue?[13]
She'll ne'er forget your parting kiss,
(*With a smile.*) Nor round her neck how fast you clung:
Nor how you with me[14] you sued to stay,
Nor how your suit your Sire forbad;
(*With agony.*) Nor how . . . (*With a look of terror.*) I'll drive such thoughts away;
(*In a hollow hurried voice.*)

They'll make me mad! They'll make me mad!
(*A pause—she then proceeds with a melancholy smile,*)
His rosy lips, how sweet They smiled!
His mild blue eyes, how bright They shone!
None ever bore a lovelier child!—[15]
(*With a sudden burst of passionate grief, approaching to frenzy.*)

And art Thou now for ever gone,
And must I never see thee more,
My pretty, pretty, pretty Lad!

---

[11] The Larpent and *Memoirs* versions have a slightly different version of this passage: "'Tis sure a dream?—some fancy vain!/I—I, the child of rank and wealth!/Am I the wretch who clanks this chain,/Deprived of freedom, friends and health?/Oh, while I count those blessings fled,/Which never more my hours must glad,/How aches my heart!—how burns my head!—'"

[12] The Larpent and *Memoirs* versions have "Ah! hast thou not forgot by this."

[13] The Larpent and *Memoirs* versions have "The mother's" twice. The various versions have differing pronouns throughout this and other passages. Lewis seems to be playing with the movement from first to third person as an indication of the Captive's madness, as she now views her position objectively or abstractly, now identifies herself with her fate, now knows who and what she is, now feels alienated from herself.

[14] The Larpent and *Memoirs* versions have "with her."

[15] The Larpent and *Memoirs* versions have "Was never born a lovelier child."

(*With energy.*) I *will* be free! (*Endeavoring to force the grate.*)
    Unbar the[16] door!
I am not mad! I am not mad!
(*She falls, exhausted, against the grate, by the bars of which she supports herself. She is roused from her stupor by loud shrieks, rattling of chains, etc.*)
Oh! Hark!—what mean those yells and cries?[17]
(*The noise grows louder.*)
His chain some furious madman breaks!—
(*The Madman is seen to rush along the gallery with a blazing firebrand in his hand.*)
He comes!—I see his glaring eyes!—
(*The madman appears at the grate, which he endeavors to force, while she shrinks in an agony of terror.*)
    Now, now my dungeon-grate He shakes!—[18]
Help, help!
(*Scared by her cries, the madman quits the grate.[19] The madman again appears above, is seized by his keepers, with torches; and after some resistance, is dragged away.*)
    He's gone!—Oh! fearful woe,
    Such screams to hear, such sights to see!
My brain, my brain!—I know, I know,
    I *am* not mad . . . but soon *shall* be!
Yes! Soon!—For Lo yon?! . . . while I speak . . .
    Mark, how yon Daemon's[20] eye balls glare!—
He see me!—Now with dreadful shriek
    He whirls a serpent[21] high in air!—
Horror!—The Reptile strikes his tooth

. . . .

[16]The Larpent and *Memoirs* versions have "this."
[17]The Larpent and *Memoirs* versions have "Hark! hark!—what mean those yells—those cries!"
[18]The *Memoirs* has "dungeon bars"; the Larpent version has "he breaks."
[19]Every account of the performance of the play notes the horrifying effect it had, with women fainting and the entire house in an uproar. The *Monthly Mirror* (15 April 1803) identifies this particular moment as the most shocking, claiming that "The effect was too strong for the feelings of the audience. Two ladies fell into hysterics, the house was thrown into confusion . . ."
[20]The *Memoirs* version has "Mark yonder demon's," Larpent "Mark yonder Damon's."
[21]The Larpent and *Memoirs* versions have "scorpion."

Deep in my heart so crush'd and sad!—
Aye,[22] laugh, ye Fiends!—I feel the truth!
    Your task is done![23] —(*With a loud shriek.*) I'm mad! I'm mad![24]
    [My Child!—My Child!—][25]

[22]The Larpent version has "Yes."
[23]The Larpent and *Memoirs* versions have "Tis done! 'tis done!"
[24]The version in *Poems* ends here.
[25]This line is in the Larpent version, which lacks all stage directions and which thus ends here; this may merely be her final recognition of her child embedded in the stage directions in the *Memoirs* version.

Caste

Thomas William Robertson
1867

Scene: London

Dramatic
> The Marchioness: a woman of means, 50s

> When she learns that her son, an army captain, is about to be posted to India, the
> Marchioness pays him a visit and offers the following advice.

MARCHIONESS: And now, my dear boy, before you go I want to
give you some advice; and you mustn't despise it because I'm an old
woman. We old women know a great deal more than people give us
credit for. You are a soldier—so was your father—so was his father—
so was mine—so was our royal founder; we were born to lead! The
common people expect it from us. It is our duty. Do you not remember in the Chronicles of Froissart? (*With great enjoyment.*) I think I can
quote it word for word; I've a wonderful memory for my age. (*With
closed eyes.*) It was in the fifty-ninth chapter—"How Godefroy
D'Alroy helde the towne of St. Amande duryng the siege before
Tournay. It said the towne was not closed but with pales. And cap-
tayne there was Sir Amory of Pauy—The Seneschall of Carcas-
soune—who had said it was not able to hold agaynste an hooste,
when one Godefroy D'Alroy sayd that rather than he woulde depart,
he woulde keep it to the best of his power. Whereat the souldiers
cheered and sayd, 'Lead us on, Sir Godefroy.' And then began a
fierce assault and they within were chased, and sought for shelter
from street to street. But Godefroy stood at the gate so valyantly that
the souldiers helde the towne until the commyng of the Earl of Hay-
nault with twelve thousand men."
[*GEORGE (Aside.*): I wish she'd go. If she once gets on to Froissart,
she'll never know when to stop.]
MARCHIONESS: When my boy fights—and you will fight—he is
sure to distinguish himself. It is his nature to—(*Toys with his hair.*)—
he cannot forget his birth. And when you meet these Asiatic ruffians,
who have dared to revolt, and to outrage humanity, you will strike as
your ancestor Sir Galtier of Chevrault struck at Poictiers. (*Changing*

tone of voice as if remembering.) Froissart mentions it thus—"Sir Galtier, with his four squires, was in the front of that battell, and there did marvels in arms., And Sir Galtier rode up to the Prince, and sayd to him—"Sir, take your horse and ryde forth, this journey is yours. God is this day in your hands. Gette us to the French Kyng's batayle. I think verily by his valyantesse he woll not fly. Advance banner in the name of God and of Saynt George!" And Sir Galtier galloped forward to see his Kynge's victory, and meet his own death."

[*GEORGE* (*Aside*.): If Esther hears all this!]

MARCHIONESS: There is another subject about which I should have spoken to you before this; but an absurd prudery forbade me. I may never see you more. I am old—and you—are going into battle—(*Kissing his forehead with emotion*.)—and this may be our last meeting. (*A noise heard within folding-doors*.) What's that?

[*GEORGE:* Nothing—my man Dixon in there.]

MARCHIONESS: We may not meet again on this earth. I do not fear your conduct, my George, with men; but I know the temptations that beset a youth who is well born. But a true soldier, a true gentleman, should not only be without fear, but without reproach. It is easier to fight a furious man than to forego the conquest of a love-sick girl. A thousand Sepoys slain in battle cannot redeem the honour of a man who has betrayed the confidence of a trusting woman. Think, George, what dishonour—what stain upon your manhood—to hurl a girl to shame and degradation! And what excuse for it? That she is plebeian? A man of real honour will spare the woman who has confessed her love for him, as he would give quarter to an enemy he had disarmed. (*Taking his hands*.) Let my boy avoid the snares so artfully spread; and when he asks his mother to welcome the woman he has chosen for his wife, let me take her to my arms and plant a motherly kiss upon the white brow of a lady. (*Noise of a fall heard within folding-doors; rising*.) What's that?

The Castle Spectre

Matthew G. Lewis
1797

Scene: England

Dramatic

Angela: a young woman longing for simpler times, 20s

Although Angela is being courted by the wealthy Osmond, she finds no sub-
stance in his lavish gifts and pines instead for the unencumbered days of her
youth.

ANGELA: Oh! my good Lord, esteem me not ungrateful! I acknowledge your bounties, but they have not made me happy. I still linger
in thought near those scenes where I passed the blessed period of infancy; I still thirst for those simple pleasures which habit has made to
me most dear. The birds which my own hands reared, and the flowers which my own hands planted; the banks on which I rested when
fatigued, the wild tangled wood which supplied me with strawber-
ries, and the village church where I prayed to be virtuous, while I yet
knew of vice and virtue but the name, all have acquired rights to my
memory and my love!

[*OSMOND:* What! these costly dresses, these scenes of pomp and
greatness—]

ANGELA: Dazzle my eyes, but leave my heart unsatisfied. What I
would meet with is affection, not respect; I had rather be obliged
than obeyed; and all these glittering gems are far less dear to me,
than one flower of a wreath which Edwy's hand have woven.

[*OSMOND:* Confusion!]

ANGELA: While I saw you, Cheviot Hills, I was happy, Oh! how
happy!

"While I listened to your artless accents, friends of my childhood,
how swelled my fond heart with gratitude and pleasure. At morn
when I left my bed, light were my spirits, and gay as the zephyrs[26] of
summer; and when at night my head again pressed my pillow, I

....

[26]Winds from the west, from Zephyros, Greek god of the west wind.

whispered to myself, 'Happy has been to-day, and to-morrow will be as happy!' Then sweet was my sleep; and my dreams were of those whom I loved dearest."

The Cenci

Percy Bysshe Shelley
1820

Scene: 16th century Rome

#1—Dramatic
> Beatrice: Unhappy daughter of the evil Count Cenci, 20s

> Beatrice once loved Orsino, who has since taken the vows of priesthood. When he continues to make romantic advances, she quickly rebuffs him.

BEATRICE: As I have said, speak not of love;
Had you a dispensation, I have not;
Nor will I leave this home of misery
Whilst my poor Bernard, and that gentle lady
To whom I owe life and these virtuous thoughts,
Must suffer what I still have strength to share.
Alas, Orsino! all the love that once
I felt for you, is turned to bitter pain.
Ours was a youthful contract, which you first
Broke, by assuming vows no Pope will loose.
And thus I love you still, but holily,
Even as a sister or a spirit might;
And so I swear a cold fidelity.
And it is well perhaps we shall not marry.
You have a sly, equivocating vein
That suits me not. Ah, wretched that I am!
Where shall I turn? Even now you look on me
As you were not my friend, and as if you
Discovered that I thought so, with false smiles
Making my true suspicion seem your wrong.
Ah! No, forgive me; sorrow makes me seem
Sterner than else my nature might have been;
I have a weight of melancholy thoughts.
And they forebode,—but what can they forebode
Worse than I now endure?
[*ORSINO:* All will be well.
Is the petition yet prepared? You know

My zeal for all you wish, sweet Beatrice;
Doubt not but I will use my utmost skill,
So that the Pope attend to your complaint.]
BEATRICE: Your zeal for all I wish;—Ah me, you are cold!
Your utmost skill—speak but one word—(*Aside*.) Alas!
Weak and deserted creature that I am,
Here I stand bickering with my only friend!
(*To Orsino*.) This night my father gives a sumptuous feast,
Orsino; he has heard some happy news
From Salamanca, from my brothers there,
And with this outward show of love he mocks
His inward hate. 'Tis bold hypocrisy,
For he would gladlier celebrate their deaths,
Which I have heard him pray for on his knees:
Great God! that such a father should be mine!
But there is mighty preparation made,
And all our kin, the Cenci, will be there,
And all the chief nobility of Rome.
And he has bidden me and my pale mother
Attire ourselves in festival array.
Poor lady! She expects some happy change
In his dark spirit from this act; I none.
At supper I will give you the petition:
Till when—farewell.

#2—Dramatic
    Beatrice

> When her father causes the deaths of her brothers, the evil man hosts a feast to
> celebrate. Here, desperate Beatrice begs the gathered lords of Rome to save her
> from her father's insane bloodlust.

BEATRICE: I do entreat you, go not, noble guests;
What, although tyranny and impious hate
Stand sheltered by a father's hoary hair?
What, if 'tis he who clothed us in these limbs
Who tortures them, and triumphs? What, if we,
The desolate and the dead, were his own flesh,
His children and his wife, whom he is bound

To love and shelter? Shall we therefore find
No refuge in this merciless wide world?
Oh, think what deep wrongs must have blotted out
First love, then reverence in a child's prone mind,
Till it thus vanquish shame and fear! O, think!
I have borne much, and kissed the sacred hand
Which crushed us to the earth, and thought its stroke
Was perhaps some paternal chastisement!
Have excused much, doubted; and when no doubt
Remained, have sought by patience, love and tears,
To soften him; and when this could not be,
I have knelt down through the long sleepless nights,
And lifted up to God, the father of all,
Passionate prayers: and when these were not heard
I have still borne;—until I meet you here,
Princes and kinsmen, at this hideous feast
Given at my brothers' deaths. Two yet remain,
His wife remains and I, whom if ye save not,
Ye may soon share such merriment again
As fathers make over their children's graves.
Oh! Prince Colonna, thou art our near kinsman;
Cardinal, thou art the Pope's chamberlain;
Camillo, thou art chief justiciary; Take us away.

The Climbers

Clyde Fitch
1901

Scene: a funeral

Dramatic

Ruth: a woman mourning the death of her brother, 30-40

Years of frustration with her brother's social-climbing wife finally erupt in an angry confrontation with her at his funeral.

RUTH (*Outraged.*): Send your daughters out of the room; I wish to answer you alone.

[*MRS. HUNTER (Frightened.*): No! What you have to say to me I prefer my children to hear! (*Clara puts her arm about her.*)]

RUTH: I can't remain quiet any longer. George— (*She almost breaks down.*) This funeral is enough, with its show and worldliness! I don't believe there was a soul in the church you didn't see! Look at your handkerchief! Real grief isn't measured by the width of a black border. I'm ashamed of you, Florence! I never liked you very much, although I tried to for your husband's sake, but now I'm even more ashamed of you. My dear brother is gone, and there need be no further bond between us, but I want you to understand the true reason why, from today, I keep away from you. This funeral was revolting to me!—a show spectacle, a social function, and for *him* who you know *hated* the very thing. (*She stops for a moment.*) I saw the reporters there, and I heard your message to them, and I contradicted it. I begged them not to use your information, and they were gentlemen and promised me not to. You are, and always have been, a silly, frivolous woman. I don't doubt you loved your husband as much as you could any man, but it wasn't enough for me; he was worth being adored by the best and noblest woman in the world. I've stood by all these years, trying with my love and silent sympathy to be some comfort to him—but I saw the disappointment and disillusionment eat away the very hope of happiness out of his heart. I tried to help him by helping you in your foolish ambitions, doing what I could to give my brother's wife the social position *his name* entitled her to!

[*MRS. HUNTER:* That's not true; I've had to fight it out all alone!]

RUTH: It was not my fault if my best friends found you intolerable; *I* couldn't blame them. Well, now it's over! George is at rest, please God. You are a rich woman to do what you please. Go, and do it! And Heaven forgive you for ruining my brother's life! I'm sorry to have said all this before your children.

Danton's Death

Georg Buchner, tr. by Henry J. Schmidt
1835

Scene: Paris during the Reign of Terror

Dramatic
> Marion: a grisette, 30s

> Here, as they tarry in bed, the earthy Marion tells Danton of her first lover, his
> death and the awakening of her endless longing.

MARION: No, let me be. Here at your feet. I want to tell you a story.
[*DANTON:* You could use your lips in better ways.]
MARION: No, let me stay like this. My mother was a smart woman,
she always said chastity was a fine virtue—when people came to the
house and started talking about certain things, she told me to leave
the room; when I asked what they wanted, she said I ought to be
ashamed of myself; when she gave me a book to read, I almost always had to skip a few pages. But I read the Bible whenever I liked—
there everything was holy; but there were things in there that I didn't
understand, and I didn't want to ask anyone; I brooded about them
by myself. Then spring came, and all around me things were going
on that I didn't take part in. I found myself in a strange atmosphere,
it almost choked me; I looked at my body, sometimes I felt I was double and then melted again into one. At that time a young man came
to our house—he was good-looking and often said crazy things; I
wasn't sure what he wanted, but I had to laugh. My mother invited
him often—both he and I liked that. Finally we couldn't see why we
might not just as well lie together between two sheets as sit next to
each other in two chairs. I enjoyed that more than our conversations,
and I didn't understand why one would allow the smaller pleasure
and deny the greater one. We did it secretly. It went on like that. But
I became like an ocean, consuming everything and swirling deeper
and deeper. For me there was only one opposite: all men melted into
one body. That was my nature—who can escape it? Finally he real-
ized it. He came one morning and kissed me as if he wanted to choke
me, his arms wrapped tight around his neck. I was terribly afraid.
Then he let me go and laughed and said he had almost done a foolish

thing, I ought to keep my dress and use it, it would wear out by itself, he didn't want to spoil my fun just yet, it was all I had. Then he left, and again I didn't know what he wanted. That evening I was sitting at the window; I'm very sensitive, and I relate to everything around me only through feeling. I became absorbed in the waves of the sunset. Then a group of people came down the street, children in front, women looking out of their windows. I looked down—they were carrying him by in a basket, the moon shone on his pale forehead, his hair was damp, he had drowned himself. I had to cry. That was the only break in my being. Other people have Sundays and working days, they work for six days and pray on the seventh; once a year, on their birthdays, they get sentimental, and every year on New Year's Day they reflect. I don't understand all that. For me there is no stopping, no changing. I'm always the same, an endless longing and grasping, a fire, a torrent. My mother died of grief, people point at me. That's silly. It's all the same feeling; whoever enjoys the most prays the most.

[*DANTON:* Why can't I contain your beauty in me completely, surround it entirely?]

MARION. Danton, your lips have eyes.

Don Juan

James Elroy Flecker
1910–11

Scene: Spain

#1—Dramatic
    Anna

> Anna's unrequited passion for Don Juan has driven her nearly mad. Here, she confronts her sister and the Don as they plan their future together. Their happiness is more than Anna can bear, and here she tells them a dark tale ending in threats.

ANNA: Smile then, children, hand in hand,
Bright and white as the summer snow,
Or that young king of the Grecian land,
Who smiled on Thetis, long ago,
So long ago, when, heart aflame,
The grave and gentle Peleus came
To the shore where the Halcyon flies,
To wed the maiden of his devotion,
The dancing lady with sky blue eyes,
Thetis, the darling of Paradise,
The daughter of old Ocean.
Seas before her rise and break,
Dolphins tumble in her wake
Along the sapphire courses.
With tritons ablow on their pearly shells,
With a plash of waves and a clash of bells,
From the glimmering house where her father dwells
She drives his white-tail horses!
And the boys of heaven gowned and crowned
Have Aphrodite to lead them round,
Aphrodite with hair unbound
Her silver breasts adorning,
Her long, her soft, her streaming hair,
Falls on her silver breasts laid bare,
By the stir and swing of the sealit air
And the movement of the morning.

(*Starting back from them.*)
But this was long ago: and now
It's night: and there has come
One with a bent and bitter brow,
A ruin for the home,
One whom no beauty graced, who had not known
A lover, save of stone,
One who in viper lairs for long years hidden
To your feast came unbidden,
One at whose breast lay doom,
A prophetess to find her father's tomb.
(*To Don Juan.*)
Was he not dear, young lover,
Was he not wise and old?
To you did he not discover
His heart, and a heart all gold,
(*Pointing to window.*)
At night beside that river
Where silently it rolled?
(*With hatred.*)
Give me the murderer visible
On whose dark face the stamp of hell
Is branded clear and cold;
But evil that with beauty blends
For a daughter's fall and the death of friends
This is a plague untold.

#2—Dramatic
Anna: an intense and passionate woman, 20s

Anna is the sister of Isabella, who is to marry Don Juan. Here, she makes a star-
tling confession to her sister's fiancé.

ANNA: Did you but know
The one brave moment of my life!
[*DON JUAN:* What was it?]
ANNA: The moment when you stooped to kiss my lips.
[*DON JUAN:* Anna! (*Offers to kiss her.*)]
Anna: No, not again. Forgive me, sir,

I have loved beauty with a plain girl's passion.
Once statues filled my eyes with it, and poems
Bent with their wings of wonder round my head
I made my soul a garden and walked therein
Like a tall Isolde; watching for the ship.
Then, all my thoughts were flowers: but *you* came,
You kissed me, and they withered. No more dreams.
I know your eyes are worth all poetry,
Your speech the whole of music faint and far,
For not the joy of Earth's remote clear mountains,
Arcadian meadow, river-threaded plain,
Not morning and the flames of all her fountains,
Not evening when she breaks in silver rain,
O not the murmur of those austral isles
Poised like red lilies on a sea that smiles,
Not all the choirs of all the sons of heaven
Shouting for joy because the stars are fire.

The Easiest Way

Eugene Walter
1908

Scene: New York City

#1—Dramatic
   Elfie: A woman of considerable experience, 30s

   When Elfie discovers that a young friend has lost her heart to a man, she delivers
   the following sobering sermons.

ELFIE (Throws cigarette into fireplace.): I don't know, don't I? I don't
know, I suppose, that when I came to this town from up state—a little burg name Oswego—and joined a chorus, that I didn't fall in love
with just such a man. I suppose I don't know that then I was the best-
looking girl in New York, and everybody talked about me? I suppose
I don't know that there were men, all ages and with all kinds of
money, ready to give me anything for the mere privilege of taking
me out to supper? And I didn't do it, did I? For three years I stuck by
this good man who was to lead me in a good way toward a good life.
And all the time I was getting older, never quite so pretty one day as
I had been the day before. I never knew then what it was to be tin
kered with by hairdressers and manicures or a hundred and one of
those other people who make you look good. I didn't have to have
them then. *(Rises, goes to table, facing Laura.)* Well, you know, Laura,
what happened.
[LAURA: Wasn't it partly your fault, Elfie?]
ELFIE (Speaking across table angrily.): Was it my fault that time made
me older and I took on a lot of flesh? Was it my fault that the work
and the life took out the color, and left the make-up? Was it my fault
that other pretty young girls came along, just as I'd come, and were
chased after, just as I was? Was it my fault the cabs weren't waiting
any more and people didn't talk about how pretty I was? And was it
my fault when he finally had me alone, and just because no one else
wanted me, he got tired and threw me flat—cold flat *(Brings hand
down on table.)* —and I'd been on the dead level with him. *(With almost a sob goes to bureau, powders nose, returns to table.)* It almost broke
my heart. Then I made up my mind to get even and get all I could

out of the game. Jerry came along. He was a has-been and I was on the road to be. He wanted to be good to me, and I let him. That's all.

#2—Dramatic
    Elfie

ELFIE: I don't see anything impossible. From all you've said to me about this fellow there is only one thing to do.
[*LAURA:* One thing?]
ELFIE: Yes—get married quick. You say he has the money and you have the love, and you're sick of Brockton, and you want to switch and do it in the decent, respectable, conventional way, and he's going to take you away. Haven't you got sense enough to know that once you're married to Mr. Madison that Will Brockton wouldn't dare go to him, and if he did Madison wouldn't believe him. A man will believe a whole lot about his girl, but nothing about his wife.
[*LAURA* (*Turns and looks at her. There is a long pause.*): Elfie (*Goes to table.*) —I—I don't think I could do like that to John. I don't think—I could deceive him.]
ELFIE: You make me sick. The thing to do is to lie to all men (*Rise, pushes chair to table.*) —they all lie to you. Protect yourself. You seem to think that your happiness depends on this. Now do it. Listen. (*Touches Laura to make her sit down; Laura sits right of table; Elfie sits on arm of chair left of table, elbows on table.*) Don't you realize that you and me, and all the girls that are shoved into this life, are practically the common prey of any man who happens to come along? Don't you know that they've got about as much consideration for us as they have for any pet animal around the house, and the only way that we've got it on the animal is that we've got brains. This is a game, Laura, not a sentiment. Do you suppose this Madison (*Laura turns to Elfie.*) —now don't get sore—hasn't turned these tricks himself before he met you, and I'll gamble he's done it since. A man's natural trade is a heartbreaking business. Don't tell me about women breaking men's hearts. The only thing they can ever break is their bankroll. And besides, this is not Will's business; he has no right to interfere. You've been with him—yes, and he's been nice to you; but I don't think that he's given you any the best of it. Now if you want to leave and go your own way and marry any Tom, Dick, or Harry that you

want, it's nobody's affair but yours.

[*LAURA:* But you don't understand—it's John. I can't lie to him.]

ELFIE: Well, that's too bad about you. I used to have that truthful habit myself, and the best I ever got was the worst of it. All this talk about love and loyalty and constancy is fine and dandy in a book, but when a girl has to look out for herself, take it from me, whenever you've got that trump card up your sleeve just play it and rake in the pot. (*Takes Laura's hand affectionately.*) You know, dearie, you're just about the only one in the world I love.

[*LAURA:* Elfie!]

ELFIE: Since I broke away from the folks up state and they've heard things, there ain't any more letters coming to me with an Oswego postmark. Ma's gone, and the rest don't care. You're all I've got in the world, Laura, and what I'm asking you to do is because I want to see you happy. I was afraid this thing was coming off, and the thing to do now is to grab your happiness, no matter how you get it nor where it comes from. There ain't a whole lot of joy in this world for you and me and the others we know, and what little you get you've got to take when you're young, because when those gray hairs begin to come, and the make-up isn't going to hide the wrinkles, unless you're well fixed it's going to be hell. You know what a fellow doesn't know doesn't hurt him, and he'll love you just the same and you'll love him. As for Brockton, let him get another girl; there're plenty 'round. Why, if this chance came to me I'd tie a can to Jerry so quick that you could hear it rattle all the way down Broadway. (*Rises, crosses back of table to Laura, leans over back of chair, and puts arms around her neck very tenderly.*) Dearie, promise me that you won't be a damn fool.

The Feast at Solhoug

Henrik Ibsen
1856

Scene: Solhoug, Norway, 14th century

#1—Serio-Comic
    Margit: an unhappy wife, 22

> On the eve of her anniversary feast, Margit finds herself in a melancholy mood. Here, she takes stock of her marriage and reveals that she feels trapped in a "gilded cage."

MARGIT: (*Sinks down on a chair by the table on the right.*)
'Twas well he departed. While here he remains
Meseems the blood freezes within my veins;
Meseems that a crushing might and cold
My heart in its clutches doth still enfold.
(*With tears she cannot repress.*)
He is my husband! I am his wife!
How long, how long lasts a woman's life?
Sixty years, mayhap—God pity me
Who am not yet full twenty-three!
(*More calmly after a short silence.*)
Hard, so long in a gilded cage to pine;
Hard a hopeless prisoner's lot—and mine.
(*Absently fingering the ornaments on the table, and beginning to put them on.*)
With rings, and with jewels, and all of my best
By his order myself I am decking—
But oh, if to-day were my burial-feast,
'Twere little that I'd be recking. (*Breaking off.*)
But if thus I brood I must needs despair;
I know a song that can lighten care. (*She sings.*)

The Hill-King to the sea did ride;
    —Oh, sad are my days and dreary—
To woo a maiden to be his bride.
    —I am waiting for thee, I am weary.—

The Hill-King rode to Sir Håkon's hold;
    —Oh, sad are my days and dreary—
Little Kirsten sat combing her locks of gold.
    —I am waiting for thee, I am weary.—

The Hill King wedded the maiden fair;
    —Oh, sad are my days and dreary—
A silvern girdle she ever must wear.
    —I am waiting for thee, I am weary.—

The Hill-King wedded the lily-wand,
    —Oh, sad are my days and dreary—
With fifteen gold rings on either hand.
    —I am waiting for thee, I am weary.—

Three summers passed, and there passed full five;
    —Oh, sad are my days and dreary—
In the hill little Kirsten was buried alive.
    —I am waiting for thee, I am weary.—

Five summers passed, and there passed full nine;
    —Oh, sad are my days and dreary—
Little Kirsten ne'er saw the glad sunshine.
    —I am waiting for thee, I am weary.—

In the dale there are flowers and the birds' blithe song;
    —Oh, sad are my days and dreary—
In the hill there is gold and the night is long
    —I am waiting for thee, I am weary.—
(*She rises and crosses the room.*)
How oft in the gloaming would Gudmund sing
This song in my father's hall.
There was somewhat in it—some strange, sad thing
That took my heart in thrall;
Though I scarce understood, I could ne'er forget—
And the words and the thoughts they haunt me yet.
(*Stops horror-struck.*)

Rings of red gold! And a belt beside—!
'Twas with gold the Hill-King wedded his bride!
(*In despair; sinks down on a bench beside the table on the left.*)
Woe! Woe! I myself am the Hill-King's wife!
And there cometh none to free me from the prison of my life.

#2—Serio-Comic
    Signë: Margit's younger sister, 18–20

> Signë is an energetic young woman who here bursts into her sister's chamber and tells her that Gudmund, their childhood friend upon whom they both had crushes is coming to the feast.

SIGNË: 'Twas early morn, and the church bells rang,
To Mass I was fain to ride;
The birds in the willows twittered and sang,
In the birch-groves far and wide.
All earth was glad in the clear, sweet day;
And from church it had well-nigh stayed me;
For still, as I rode down the shady way,
Each rosebud beguiled and delayed me.
Silently into the church I stole;
The priest at the altar was bending;
He chanted and read, and with awe in their soul,
The folk to God's word were attending.
Then a voice rang out o'er the fiord so blue;
And the carven angels, the whole church through,
Turned round, methought, to listen thereto.
[*MARGIT:* O Signë, say on! Tell me all, tell me all!]
SIGNË: 'Twas as though a strange, irresistible call
Summoned me forth from the worshipping flock,
Over hill and dale, over mead and rock.
'Mid the silver birches I listening trod,
Moving as though in a dream;
Behind me stood empty the house of God;
Priest and people were lured by the magic, 'twould seem,
Of the tones that still through the air did stream.
No sound they made; they were quiet as death;
To hearken the song-birds held their breath,

The lark dropped earthward, the cuckoo was still,
As the voice re-echoed from hill to hill.
[*MARGIT:* Go on.]
SIGNË: They crossed themselves, women and men;
(*Pressing her hands to her breast.*)
But strange thoughts arose within me then;
For the heavenly song familiar grew:
Gudmund oft sang it to me and you—
Ofttimes has Gudmund carolled it,
And all he e'er sang in my heart is writ.
[*MARGIT:* And you think that it may be—?]
SIGNË: I know it! I know it! You soon shall see!
(*Laughing.*)
From far-off lands, at the last, in the end,
Each song-bird homewards his flight doth bend!
I am so happy—though why I scarce know—!
Margit, what say you? I'll quickly go
And take down his harp, that has hung so long
In there on the wall that 'tis rusted quite;
Its golden strings I will polish bright,
And tune them to ring and to sing with his song.
[*MARGIT* (*Absently.*): Do as you will—]
SIGNË (*Reproachfully.*): Nay, this is not right. (*Embracing her.*)
But when Gudmund comes will your heart grow light—
Light, as when I was a child, again.
[*MARGIT* (*To herself.*): So much has changed—ah, so much!—since
then—]
SIGNË: Margit, you shall be happy and gay!
Have you not serving-maids many, and thralls?
Costly robes hang in rows on your chamber walls;
How rich you are, none can say.
By day you can ride in the forest deep,
Chasing the hart and the hind;
By night in a lordly bower you can sleep,
On pillows of silk reclined.

Margit and Gudmund were once secret lovers. Gudmund deserted Margit to pursue another woman, and Margit has never forgiven him. In fact, Margit blames Gudmund for her unhappy married life. At the feast, the guests demand that Margit entertain them all with a tale. Driven to desperation by Gudmund's presence, Margit impetuously tells her own sad story, and then collapses.

MARGIT: It was a fair and noble maid,

She dwelt in her father's hall;

Both linen and silk did she broider and braid,

Yet found in it solace small.

For she sat there alone in cheerless state,

Empty were hall and bower;

In the pride of her heart, she was fain to mate

With a chieftain of pelf and power.

But now 'twas the Hill-King, he rode from the north,

With his henchmen and his gold;

On the third day at night he in triumph fared forth,

Bearing her to his mountain hold.

Full many a summer she dwelt in the hill;

Out of beakers of gold she could drink at her will.

Oh, fair are the flowers of the valley, I trow,

But only in dreams can she gather them now!

'Twas a youth, right gentle and gold to boot,

Struck his harp with such magic might

That it rang to the mountain's inmost root,

Where she languished in the night.

The sound in her soul waked a wondrous mood—

Wide open the mountain-gates seemed to stand;

The peace of God lay over the land,

And she saw how it all was fair and good.

There had happened what never had happened before;

She had wakened to life as his harp-strings thrilled;

And her eyes were opened to all the store

Of treasure wherewith the good earth is filled.

For mark this well: it hath ever been found

that those who in caverns deep lie bound

Are lightly freed by the harp's glad sound.

He saw her prisoned, he heard her wail—
But he cast unheeding his harp aside,
Hoisted straightway his silken sail,
And sped away o'er the waters wide
To stranger strands with his new-found bride.
(*With ever increasing passion.*)
So fair was thy touch on the golden strings
That my breast heaves high and my spirit sings!
I must out, I must out to the sweet green leas!
I die in the Hill-King's fastnesses!
He mocks at my woe as he clasps his bride
And sails away o'er the waters wide! (*Shrieks.*)
With me all is over; my hill-prison barred;
Unsunned is the day, and the night all unstarred.
(*She totters and, fainting, seeks to support herself against the trunk of a tree.*)

#4—Dramatic
   Margit

   Following her collapse, Margit recovers in her bed chamber, her thoughts on
   Gudmund and suicide.

MARGIT: To-morrow, then, Gudmund will ride away
Out into the world so great and wide.
Alone with my husband here I must stay;
And well do I know what will then betide.
Like the broken branch and the trampled flower
I shall suffer and fade from hour to hour.
(*Short pause; she leans back in her chair.*)
I once heard a tale of a child blind from birth,
Whose childhood was full of joy and mirth;
For his mother, with spells of magic might,
Wove for the dark eyes a world of light.
And the child looked forth with wonder and glee
Upon valley and hill, upon land and sea.
Then suddenly the witchcraft failed—
The child once more was in darkness pent;
Good-bye to games and merriment;

With longing vain the red cheeks paled.
And its wail of woe, as it pined away,
Was ceaseless, and sadder than words can say.—
Oh! like that child's my eyes were sealed,
To the light and the life of summer blind—
(*She springs up.*)
But now—! And I in this cage confined!
No, now is the worth of my youth revealed!
Three years of life I on him have spent—
My husband—but were I longer content
This hapless, hopeless weird to dree,
Meek as a dove I needs must be.
I am wearied to death of petty brawls;
The stirring life of the great world calls.
I will follow Gudmund with shield and bow,
I will share his joys, I will soothe his woe,
Watch o'er him both by night and day.
All that behold shall envy the life
Of the valiant knight and Margit his wife.—
His wife! (*Wrings her hands.*)
Oh God, what is this I say!
Forgive me, forgive me, and oh! let me feel
The peace that hath power both to soothe and to heal.
(*Walks back and forward, brooding silently.*)
Signë, my sister—? How hateful 'twere
To steal her glad young life from her!
But who can tell? In very sooth
She may love him but with the light love of youth.
(*Again silence; she takes out the little phial, looks long at it and says under
her breath:*)
This phial—were I its powers to try—
My husband would sleep for ever and aye!
(*Horror-struck.*)
No, no! To the river's depths with it straight!
(*In the act of throwing it out of the window, stops.*)
And yet I could—'tis not yet too late.—
(*With an expression of mingled horror and rapture, whispers.*)

With what a magic resistless might
Sin masters us in our own despite!
Doubly alluring methinks is the goal
I must reach through blood, with the wreck of my soul.
(*Bengt, with the empty beaker in his hand, comes in from the passage-way; his face is red; he staggers slightly.*)

Gyges and His Ring

Friedrich Hebbel, tr. by Marion W. Sonnenfeld
1856

Scene: the kingdom of Lydia

Dramatic

Rhodope: Queen of Lydia, a woman deceived by her husband, 20–30

The king has allowed Gyges to wear a ring that renders him invisible so that his visitor may behold his beautiful wife in her most natural of states. When Rhodope discovers that she has been so violated, she falls into a deep depression and no longer wishes to live. Here, she asks the gods why they have visited so much misery upon her.

RHODOPE: Eternal gods, could this have come to pass?
I've brought you many pious offerings
With purity of heart from childhood on.
The first lock of my hair did fall to you
Before I ever knew that you held in
Your hands all blessings fit for human life.
As a young woman too, I never failed
To serve you; rarely did a wish rise up
To your high place with my burnt offering.
With modesty and fear, I sought to press
Under my consciousness each wish which might
Have just begun to stir within my heart.
Sincere was my desire just to pray
For your regard and never for your gifts;
I wanted to be grateful, not to beg.
Nor did I, as a woman, wait to be
Reminded by a dream of sacred duty
As did the daughter of the Tyndarids.
For I did decorate the altar of
My own desire. And still—why dedicate
The best part of one's goods to you
If you would not with mercy shield a man
Where he alone can not protect himself.
The lion who leaps out at hot noon time,
When rage or hunger drives him, can always be

Controlled by man with sword and courage, and
No brave man cries to Zeus for lightning then.
But that the coward snake not creep to him,
When he, exhausted after battle, sleeps,
That is your work, for night is yours alone!
And I—and I—have I been so accursed.
Accursed since birth, so that your strength is chained
Down at the Styx, so that you gave success
As to a pious deed—to sacrilege—
Against me—which no one would dare commit
Against the very lowest of my slaves?

Judith

Friedrich Hebbel, tr. by Marion W. Sonnenfeld
1840

Scene: Bethulia

Dramatic

> Judith: a woman who has vowed to free her people from Holofernes, the Tyrant of Babylon, 20s

> Judith has boldly volunteered to kill the dread Holofernes. When her goal is questioned by Ephraim, a man she despises, Judith explodes with feminist passion.

JUDITH: I see him too, with his face which is all eyes, commanding eyes, and his feet before which the earth upon which he walks seems to shrink away. But there was a time, when he was not; therefore, a time can come, when he will no longer be!

[EPHRAIM: Give him the thunder and remove his army from him, and I'll try it, but now—]

JUDITH: Just will it! And up from the depths of the abyss and down from the firmament of heaven you will summon holy, protecting forces and they will bless and shield your deeds, if not you! For you want what is universally wanted: that about which God broods in his first rage and which Nature plans while gnashing her teeth in torturing dreams, she who trembles before the gigantic creature born from her own womb and will not create the second man like him unless she does it to have him annihilate the first.

[EPHRAIM: You demand the unthinkable from me only because you hate me and want to kill me.]

JUDITH (*Glowing.*): I did not misjudge you! What's this? Such an idea does not inspire you? Doesn't even intoxicate you? I, whom you love, and who wish to raise you beyond yourself so that I should be able to return your love, I place this thought into your soul, and it means nothing to you but a burden which presses you more deeply into the dust? You see, if you had received the idea exultantly, if impulsively you had reached for your sword, and had not even taken the time for quick farewell, then, oh, I feel it, then I would have cried and thrown myself in your path; I'd have elaborated on the danger with the fear of a heart which trembles for the one it loves most; I'd have kept you from it or followed you. But now—ha! I am more than justified; your love is your punishment for your impoverished nature; it is your curse that you be consumed by it; I'd be enraged at myself if I were ever to catch myself feeling even a little sorry for you. I understand you completely, even understand that what is loftiest must seem lowest of all to you; that you must smile when I pray!

Lady Inger of Östråt

Henrik Ibsen
1855

Scene: Norway, 1528

#1—Dramatic
> Lady Inger: a woman whose life has been ruined by political intrigue, 40s

Lady Inger's allowed her first child, a son born out of wedlock to a Danish noble-man, to be taken from her in order to keep quiet a conspiracy concerning King Christian II. Years late, she is again approached to play a role in the maddeningly complex realm of Scandinavian power struggles. The price of her cooperation is the return of her son. Here, she tells the story to an old friend.

LADY INGER: Hearken, Sir Councillor! What you know you shall know thoroughly. And you too, my old and faithful friend!

Listen then. To-night you bade me call to mind that fatal day when Knut Alfson was slain at Oslo. You bade me remember the promise I made as I stood by his corpse amid the bravest men in Nor-way. I was scarce full-grown then; but I felt God's strength in me, and methought, as many have thought since, that the Lord himself had set his mark on me and chosen me to fight in the forefront for my country's cause.

Was it pride of heart? Or was it a calling from on high? That I have never clearly known. But woe to whoso is charged with a mighty task.

For seven years I fear not to say that I kept my promise faithfully. I stood by my countrymen in all their sufferings and their need. Play-mates of mine, all over the land, were wives and mothers now. I alone could give ear to no wooer—not to one. That you know best, Olaf Skaktavl!

Then I saw Sten Sture for the first time. Fairer man had never met my sight.
[*NILS LYKKE:* Ah, now it grows clear to me! Sten Sture was then in Norway on a secret errand. We Danes were not to know that he wished your friends well.]
LADY INGER: In the guise of a mean serving-man he lived a whole winter under one roof with me.

That winter I thought less and less of the country's weal. —So fair a man had I never seen—and I had lived well-nigh five-and-twenty years.

Next autumn Sten Sture came once more; and when he departed again he took with him, in all secrecy, a little child. 'Twas not folks' evil tongues I feared; but our cause would have suffered had it got abroad that Sten Sture stood so near to me.

The child was given to Peter Kanzler to rear. I waited for better times, that were soon to come. They never came. Sten Sture took a wife two years later in Sweden, and, when he died, he left a widow—

[*OLAF SKAKTAVL:* —And with her a lawful heir to his name and rights.]

LADY INGER: Time after time I wrote to Peter Kanzler beseeching him to give me back my child. But he was ever deaf to my prayers. "Cast in your lot with us once for all," he said, "and I send your son back to Norway; not before." But 'twas even that I dared not do. We of the disaffected party were then ill regarded by many timorous folk in the land. Had these learnt how things stood—oh, I know it!—to cripple the mother they had gladly meted to the child the fate that would have been King Christiern's had he not saved himself by flight![27]

But, besides that, the Danes, too, were active. They spared neither threats nor promises to force me to join them.

[*OLAF SKAKTAVL:* 'Twas but reason. The eyes of all men were fixed on you as on the vane that should show them how to shape their course.]

LADY INGER: Then came Herlof Hyttefad's rising. Do you remember that time, Olaf Skaktavl? Was it not as though a new spring had dawned over the whole land! Mighty voices summoned me to come forth;—yet I dared not. I stood doubting—far from the strife—in my lonely castle. At times it seemed as though the Lord God himself were calling me; but then would come the killing dread again to benumb my will. "Who will win?"—that was the question that was ever ringing in my ears.

'Twas but a short spring that had come to Norway. Herlof Hytte-

---

[27]King Christian II of Denmark (the perpetrator of the massacre at Stockholm known as the Blood-Bath) fled to Holland in 1523, five years before the date assigned to this play, in order to escape death or imprisonment at the hands of his rebellious nobles, who summoned his uncle, Frederick I, to the throne. Returning to Denmark in 1532, Christian was thrown in prison, where he spent the last twenty-seven years of his life.

fad, and many more with him, were broken on the wheel during the months that followed. None could call me to account; yet there lacked not covert threats from Denmark. What if they knew the secret? At last methought they must know; I knew not how else to understand their words.

'Twas even in that time of agony that Gyldenlöve, the High Steward, came hither and sought me in marriage. Let any mother anguished for her child think herself in my place!—A month after, I was the High Steward's wife—and homeless in the hearts of my countrymen.

Then came the quiet years. No one raised his head any more. Our masters might grind us down even as heavily as they listed. There were times when I loathed myself; for what had I to do? Nought but to endure terror and scorn and bring forth daughters into the world. My daughters! God must forgive me if I have had no mother's heart towards them. My wifely duties were as serfdom to me; how then could I love my daughters? Oh, how different with my son! He was the child of my very soul. He was the one thing that brought to mind the time when I was a woman and nought but a woman.—And him they had taken from me! He was growing up among strangers, who might, mayhap, be sowing in him the seed of corruption! Olaf Skaktavl—had I wandered, like you, on the lonely hills, hunted and forsaken, in winter and storm—if I had but held my child in my arms,—trust me, I had not sorrowed and wept so sore as I have sorrowed and wept for him from his birth even to this hour!

#2—Dramatic
    Lady Inger

Lady Inger has agreed to Nils Lykke's demands in order to be reunited with her son, but in doing so, renounced his right to the throne. Here, she agonizes over her decision.

LADY INGER (*After a pause.*): They call me keen-witted beyond all others in the land. I believe they are right. The keenest-witted— No one knows how I became so. For more than twenty years I have fought to save my child. That is the key to the riddle. Ay, that sharpens the wits!

My wits? Where have they flown to-night? What has become of

my forethought? There is a ringing and rushing in my ears. I see shapes before me, so lifelike that methinks I could lay hold on them. (*Springs up.*) Lord Jesus—what is this? Am I no longer mistress of my reason? Is it to come to that—? (*Presses her clasped hands over her head; sits down again, and says more calmly:*) Nay, 'tis nought. 'Twill pass. There is no fear;—it will pass.

How peaceful it is in the hall to-night! No threatening looks from forefathers or kinsfolk. No need to turn their faces to the wall. (*Rises again.*) Ay, 'twas well that I took heart at last. We shall conquer;—and then am I at the goal of all my longings. I shall have my child again. (*Takes up the light as if to go, but stops and says musingly:*) At the goal? The goal? To have him back? Is that all?—is there nought further? (*Sets the light down on the table.*) That heedless word that Nils Lykke threw forth at random—. How could he see my unborn thought?

A king's mother? A king's mother, he said— And why not? Have not my fathers before me ruled as kings, even though they bore not the kingly name? Has not my son as good a title as the other to the rights of the house of Sture? In the sight of God he has—if so be there is justice in Heaven.

And in an hour of terror I have signed away his rights. I have recklessly squandered them, as a ransom for his freedom.

If they could be recovered?— Would Heaven be angered, if I—? Would it call down fresh troubles on my head if I were to—? Who knows;— who knows! It may be safest to refrain. (*Takes up light again.*) I shall have my child again. That must content me. I will try to rest. All these desperate thoughts,—I will sleep them away. (*Goes towards the back, but stops in the middle of the hall, and says broodingly:*) A king's mother!

A Live Woman in the Mines

"Old Block" Alonzo Delano
1857

Scene: the mountains outside of Sacramento

Serio-Comic

High Betty Marlin (Betsey): a miner searching for her man, 20s

Betsey has received a letter from Jess, the man she loves, and makes up her mind to follow him into the California wilderness. She is soon lost in the mountains with her wagon and sick uncle. Here, she takes a moment to lament her desperate state.

BETSEY (*Sitting down on a rock.*): O, dear, what trouble I have in hunting up a man—come two-thousand miles and havn't found him yet; ef it had been any body else but Jess, I'd seen all the men hung first, afore I'd wore out so much shoe-leather in running arter 'em! Ef it hadn't been for him, I'd have been hoein corn and pulling flax on the plantation now, instead of climbing these hills. These pesky men do bother our heads so orfully when they do get in; thar's no getting along without one—and after all thar isn't one in a hundred that's worth the trouble they give us. Then, like a flea, thar's no sartinty of of catching one—for just as yer get yer finger on him, like as any way he's hopping off after somebody else. Let me catch Jess hoppin arter somebody else. Giminy! wouldn't I give him jessie?—wouldn't I crack him? O, Jess, Jess—you run arter somebody else! O, murder! O, ef he should? O! O! (*Weeps.*) I'm a poor, lone, lorn woman—Uncle Joe sick—lost in the mountains—and Jess, my Jess, to serve me so! My courage is gone—my boots worn out—wagon tire getting loose—my best har comb broke—all trying to find a man, and him to use me so. (*Weeps.*) It will break my heart! O! O! O! (*A gun shot is heard.*) Ha! (*Springs up and listens.*) Sluice in trouble? (*Forgets her lamentation instantly; runs to the wagon and seizes a rifle.*) Keep still, Uncle Joe—ef thar's danger, I'm ready for it.

Love's Comedy

Henrik Ibsen
1863

Scene: Norway

Dramatic
     Svanhild: a young woman rejecting a marriage proposal, 20s

   Falk, a would-be writer who rents a room from Svanhild's mother, has just proposed. Here, Svanhild turns the pompous young man down.

SVANHILD (*Lifting her head after a brief silence, looking at him and drawing nearer.*): Now I will recompense your kind intent
To save me, with an earnest admonition.
That falcon-image gave me sudden vision
What your "emancipation" really meant.
You said you were the falcon, that must fight
Athwart the wind if it would reach the sky,
I was the breeze you must be breasted by,
Else vain were all your faculty of flight;
How pitifully mean! How paltry! Nay
How ludicrous, as you yourself divined!
That seed, however, fell not by the way,
But bred another fancy in my mind
Of a far more illuminating kind.
You, as I saw it, were no falcon, but
A tuneful dragon, out of paper cut,
Whose Ego holds a secondary station,
Dependent on the string for animation;
Its breast was scrawled with promises to pay
In cash poetic,—at some future day;
The wings were stiff with barbs and shafts of wit
That wildly beat the air, but never hit;
The tail was a satiric rod in pickle
To castigate the town's infirmities,
But all it compass'd was to lightly tickle
The casual doer of some small amiss.
So you lay helpless at my feet, imploring:

"O raise me, how and where is all the same!
Give me the power of singing and of soaring,
No matter at what cost of bitter blame!"
[FALK (*Clenching his fists in inward agitation.*): Heaven be my witness—!]
SVANHILD: No, you must be told:—
For such a childish sport I am too old.
But you, whom Nature made for high endeavor,
Are you content the fields of air to tread
Hanging your poet's life upon a thread
That at my pleasure I can slip and sever?
[FALK (*Hurriedly.*): What is the date to-day?]
SVANHILD (*More gently.*): Why, now, that's right!
Mind well this day, and heed it, and beware;
Trust to your own wings only for your flight,
Sure, if they do not break, that they will bear.
The paper poem for the desk is fit,
That which is lived alone has life in it;
That only has the wings that scale the height;
Choose now between them, poet: be, or write!
(*Nearer to him.*) Now, I have done what you besought me; now
My requiem is chanted from the bough;
My only one; now all my songs are flown;
Now if you will, I'm ready for the stone!

Lucrezia Borgia

Victor Hugo, tr. by George Burnham Ives
1842

Scene: Ferrara

Dramatic

Lucrezia Borgia: a strong-willed woman, 20–30

When Lucrezia comes to believe that her husband's people are mocking her, she angrily confronts him and demands that he do something about it.

DONA LUCREZIA (Rushing into the room impetuously.): Signor, signor, this is outrageous, it is detestable, it is infamous! Some one of your subjects—do you know that, Don Alphonso?—has mutilated your wife's name carved below the arms of my family on the front of your own palace! The deed was done in broad daylight, publicly—by whom? I do not know, but 'tis most insulting and most rash! He has made my name a symbol of ignominy, and your Ferrara populace, which is the most villainous populace in Italy, signor, stands laughing about my escutcheon as about the pillory.—Can it be that you imagine, Don Alphonso, that I will submit to that, and that I would not prefer to die once by a dagger-thrust, than a thousand times by the poisoned stings of sarcasm and sneering jests? By Heaven, monsignore, I receive strange treatment in your lordship of Ferrara! I am beginning to weary of it, and methinks that you are much too benign and placid while your wife's good name is being dragged in the gutters of your city and torn to shreds by insult and calumny. I must have signal reparation for this, I forewarn you, my lord Duke. Prepare to do justice. This is a momentous thing that has happened, you see! Do you, by any chance, believe that I care nothing for the esteem of any person on earth, and that my husband can avoid being my champion? No, no, monsignore, he who weds protects. He who gives his hand, gives his arm. I rely upon you.—Every day there is some new insult, and you seem never to be moved thereby. Is it because the mud with which I am covered does not spatter you, Don Alphonso? Come, by my soul! lose your temper; let me see you, for once in your life, angry in my behalf, signor! You are in love with me, you sometimes say. In that case be in love with my renown! You are

jealous? Then be jealous of my good name! If I doubled your heredi-
tary domains by my dowry; if I brought you in marriage not only the
rose of gold and the blessing of the Holy Father, but those other
things which occupy more space on the earth's surface—Siena, Rim-
ini, Cesena, Spoleto, and Piombino, and more towns than you had
castles, and more duchies than you had baronies; if I have made of
you the most powerful noble in all Italy, that is no reason, signor,
why you should allow your people to mock at me, spread my name
abroad, and insult me; why you should allow your Ferrara to call the
attention of all Europe to your wife as being more despised and more
degraded than the maid-servant of your groom's footman; that is no
reason, I say, why your subjects cannot see me pass among them
without crying out: "Ah! that woman!"—Now, I declare to you,
signor, that I propose that the crime of to-day shall be investigated
and signally punished, or I shall complain to the Pope. I shall complain to Valentinois, who is at Forli with fifteen thousand troops; and
now consider whether it is worth while for you to rise from your
chair!

Marion de Lorme

Victor Hugo, tr. by George Burnham Ives
1831

Scene: France, 1638

Dramatic
    Marion: a woman fighting for the life of the man she loves, 20s

Didier has been found guilty of participating in a duel and has been sentenced to
death. Here, Marion desperately pleads with Louis XIII to spare his life.

MARION: Ah! may the King have pity on our grief!
Know you the truth? Two young and foolish men
Doomed by a duel to the vast abyss!
To die! great God! on a degrading gibbet!
You will have mercy on them!—I know not,
Being a woman, how one speaks to kings.
Mayhap to weep is ill; but in good sooth
Your cardinal's a veritable villain!
Why does he wish them ill? What have they done?
He has not even seen my Didier.
Alas! whoso has seen him loves him well.
—To kill them both, at their age, for a duel!
Think of their mothers! Ah! 'tis horrible!
O heaven! you will not have it so! Ah me!
We women know not how to speak like men,
We've nought but tears and shrieks, and trembling knees
The which at a king's glance give way beneath us!
That they did wrong is true; if their wrongdoing
Both you offend, forgive them. They are young.
Mon Dieu! do young men know what 'tis they do?
For a mere glance, a word, a gesture—nay,
Too often 'tis for nought—they take offence,
Wax wroth and throw away all self-control.
There's not a day this thing does not befall.
These gentlemen do know it. Ask them, Sire.—
Is it not so, messieurs?—Oh! dire misfortune!
To think that with one word you save two lives!

Oh! I will love you, Sire, if you do!
Mercy! mercy! My God! could I but speak,
Then you would say: "She must be comforted,
Poor child! Her Didier's her very soul—"
I stifle. Pity, Sire!

Mrs. Warren's Profession

George Bernard Shaw
1893

Scene: England

#1—Dramatic
    Mrs. Warren: a hard-working madam, 40s

> Mrs. Warren has supported her daughter, Vivie, by managing prostitutes. When Vivie discovers the truth about her mother's profession, she is sympathetic. Here, Mrs. Warren makes no apologies for her chosen career.

MRS. WARREN: Well, of course, dearie, it's only good manners to be ashamed of it: its expected from a woman. Women have to pretend to feel a great deal that they don't feel. Liz used to be angry with me for plumping out the truth about it. She used to say that when every woman could learn enough from what was going on in the world before her eyes, there was no need to talk about it to her. But then Liz was such a perfect lady! She had the true instinct of it; while I was always a bit of a vulgarian. I used to be so pleased when you sent me your photos to see that you were growing up like Liz: you've just her ladylike, determined way. But I can't stand saying one thing when everyone knows I mean another. What's the use in such hypocrisy? If people arrange the world that way for women, there's no good pretending it's arranged the other way. No: I never was a bit ashamed really. I consider I had a right to be proud of how we managed everything so respectably, and never had a word against us, and how the girls were so well taken care of. Some of them did very well: one of them married an ambassador. But of course now I daren't talk about such things: whatever would they think of us! (*She yawns.*) Oh dear! I do believe I'm getting sleepy after all. (*She stretches herself lazily, thoroughly relieved by her explosion, and placidly ready for her night's rest.*)

Mrs. Warren

When Vivie discovers that her mother is still a working madam, she angrily announces her intention to sever all ties with her. Here, Mrs. Warren does her best to point out to idealistic Vivie that life is hard, and to survive, you need all the help you can get.

MRS. WARREN: I mean that you're throwing away all your chances for nothing. You think that people are what they pretend to be: that the way you were taught at school and college to think right and proper is the way things really are. But it's not: it's all only a pretence, to keep the cowardly slavish common run of people quiet. do you want to find that out, like other women, at forty, when you've thrown yourself away and lost your chances; or won't you take it in good time now from your own mother, that loves and swears to you that it's truth: gospel truth? (*Urgently.*) Vivie: the big people, the clever people, the managing people, all know it. They do as I do, and think what I think. I know plenty of them. I know them to speak to, to introduce you to, to make friends of for you. I don't mean anything wrong: that's what you don't understand: your head is full of ignorant ideas about me. What do the people that taught you know about life or about people like me? When did they ever meet me, or speak to me, or let anyone tell them about me? the fools! Would they ever have done anything for you if I hadn't paid them? Havn't I told you that I want you to be respectable? Haven't I brought you up to be respectable? And how can you keep it up without my money and my influence and Lizzie's friends? Can't you see that you're cutting your own throat as well as breaking my heart in turning your back on me?

Otho the Great

John Keats
1819

Scene: Germany

Dramatic

Lady Auranthe: sister to the Duke of Franconia, 20s

Scheming Auranthe has plotted to gain the crown by marrying Otho's son. When her plotting is discovered, she fears, correctly, that the title "Empress" is now forever out of her grasp.

AURANTHE (Sola.): Down, down, proud temper!
down, Auranthe's pride!
Why do I anger him when I should kneel?
Conrad! Albert! help! help! What can I do?
O wretched woman! lost, wreck'd, swallow'd up,
Accursed, blasted! O, thou gold Crown,
Orbing along the serene firmament
Of a wide empire, like a glowing moon;
And thou, bright sceptre! lustrous in my eyes,—
There—as the fabled fair Hesperian tree,
Bearing a fruit more precious! graceful thing,
Delicate, godlike, magic! must I leave
Thee to melt in the visionary air,
Ere, by one grasp, this common hand is made
Imperial? I do not know the time
When I have wept for sorrow; but methinks
I could now sit upon the ground, and shed
Tears, tears of misery! O, the heavy day!
How shall I bear my life till Albert comes?
Ludolph! Erminia! Proofs! O heavy day!
Bring me some mourning weeds, that I may 'tire
Myself, as fits one wailing her own death:
Cut off these curls, and brand this lily hand,
And throw these jewels from my loathing sight,—
Fetch me a missal, and a string of beads,—
A cup of bitter'd water, and a crust,—

I will confess, O holy Abbot!—How!
What is this? Auranthe! thou fool, dolt,
Whimpering idiot! up! up! and quell!
I am safe! Coward! why am I in fear?
Albert! he cannot stickle, chew the cud
In such a fine extreme,—impossible!
Who knocks?

Penthesilea

Heinrich von Kleist, tr. by Martin Greenberg
1806–07

Scene: a battlefield near Troy

Dramatic
>   Penthesilea: Queen of the Amazons, 20–30

> This brave warrior woman has fallen in love with Achilles. The fact that they are
> sworn enemies in battle has driven her near to madness. As the Trojan general
> approaches, Penthesilea calls her Amazon warriors to battle.

PENTHESILEA: He's coming, good.
Dear virgins, arm, now we are called to battle!
Pass up to me the spear that throws the truest,
the sword that flashes out most lightninglike!
Gods, grant me now, you must, the bliss
of stretching in the dust, beneath my foot, this
so hotly wished-for youth of mine. All
other happiness weighed out to me
as my life's share, I cede it back to you
Asteria, I put you in command!
Keep the Greek troops busy, see to it
the violence of the fighting doesn't interfere
with me. No one here, whoever, is allowed
to strike a blow at him herself! An arrow,
death-edged, is reserved for her who dares
to lay a hand—what am I saying—
finger, on him! I, I only am
the one to bring him down. This steel I have
here, comrades, with the softest hug (since our
hugging must be done with steel), this steel
must draw him down onto my bosom, with
no pain. And flowers of the springtime, bear
him up as he sinks down so that no limb
of his will suffer hurt. Sooner would I
spare the blood out of my own heart. I'll never
rest till I have brought him down, out

of the sky like some bright-colored bird, here
to me; and when he lies with folded wings
before my feet, with not the least drop
of his royal purple lost, then let all
the Blessed Ones descend the sky to us
to celebrate our victory, then let
our march of jubilation homeward wind,
then am I your dear Queen of our Feast
of Roses! Now follow me!

Prometheus Unbound

Percy Bysshe Shelley
1820

Scene: a ravine of icy rocks in the Indian Caucasus

#1—Dramatic
   The Earth

> Here, the spirit of the Earth visits Prometheus, a man who boldly stole fire from
> the gods and who is now chained to a mountain by Zeus.

THE EARTH: I am the Earth,
Thy mother; she within whose stony veins
To the last fibre of the loftiest tree
Whose thin leaves trembled in the frozen air,
Joy ran, as blood within a living frame,
When thou didst from her bosom, like a cloud
Of glory, arise, a spirit of keen joy!
And at thy voice her pining sons uplifted
Their prostrate brows from the polluting dust,
And our almighty Tyrant with fierce dread
Grew pale, until his thunder chained thee here.
Then—see those million worlds which burn and roll
Around us—their inhabitants beheld
My spherèd light wane in wide Heaven; the sea
Was lifted by strange tempest, and new fire
From earthquake-rifted mountains of bright snow
Shook its portentous hair beneath Heaven's frown;
Lightning and Inundation vexed the plains;
Blue thistles bloomed in cities; foodless toads
Within voluptuous chambers panting crawled.
When Plague had fallen on man and beast and worm,
And Famine; and black blight on herb and grass,
Teemed ineradicable poisonous weeds
Draining their growth, for my wan breast was dry
With grief, and the thin air, my breath was stained
With the contagion of a mother's hate
Breathed on her child's destroyer; ay, I heard

Thy curse, the which, if thou rememberest now,
Yet my innumerable seas and streams,
Mountains, and caves, and winds, and yon wide air,
And the inarticulate people of the dead,
Preserve, a treasured spell. We meditate
In secret joy and hope those dreadful words,
But dare not speak them.
[*PROMETHEUS:* Venerable mother!
All else who live and suffer take from thee
Some comfort; flowers, and fruits, and happy sounds,
And love, though fleeting; these may not be mine.
But mine own words, I pray, deny me not.]
THE EARTH: They shall be told. Ere Babylon was dust,
The Magus Zoroaster, my dead child,
Met his own image walking in the garden.
That apparition, sole of men, he saw.
For know there are two worlds of life and death:
One that which thou beholdest; but the other
Is underneath the grave, where do inhabit
The shadows of all forms that think and live,
Till death unite them and they part no more;
Dreams and the light imaginings of men,
And all that faith creates or love desires,
Terrible, strange, sublime and beauteous shapes.
There thou art, and dost hang, a writhing shade,
'Mid whirlwind-peopled mountains; all the gods
Are there, and all the powers of nameless worlds,
Vast, sceptred phantoms; heroes, men, and beasts;
And Demogorgon, a tremendous gloom;
And he, the supreme Tyrant, on his throne
Of burning gold. Son, one of these shall utter
The curse which all remember. Call at will
Thine own ghost, or the ghost of Jupiter,
Hades or Typhon, or what mightier Gods
From all-profile Evil, since thy ruin,
Have sprung, and trampled on my prostrate sons.
Ask, and they must reply: so the revenge

Of the Supreme may sweep through vacant shades,
As rainy wind through the abandoned gate
Of a fallen palace.

Here, the mystical young sprite tells her sister of a strange dream.

PANTHEA: Pardon, great Sister! but my wings were faint
With the delight of a remembered dream,
As are the noontide plumes of summer winds
Satiate with sweet flowers. I was wont to sleep
Peacefully, and awake refreshed and calm,
Before the sacred Titan's fall and thy
Unhappy love had made, through use and pity,
Both love and woe familiar to my heart
As they had grown to thine: erewhile I slept
Under the glaucous caverns of old Ocean
Within dim bowers of green and purple moss,
Our young Ione's soft and milky arms
Locked then, as now, behind my dark, moist hair,
While my shut eyes and cheek were pressed within
The folded depth of her life-breathing bosom:
But not as now, since I am made the wind
Which fails beneath the music that I bear
Of thy most wordless converse; since dissolved
Into the sense with which love talks, my rest
Was troubled and yet sweet; my waking hours
Too full of care and pain.
[*ASIA:* Lift up thine eyes, and let me read thy dream.]
PANTHEA: As I have said,
With our sea-sister at his feet I slept.
The mountain mists, condensing at our voice
Under the moon, had spread their snowy flakes,
From the keen ice shielding our linked sleep.
Then two dreams came. One I remember not.
But in the other his pale wound-worn limbs
Fell from Prometheus, and the azure night

Grew radiant with the glory of that form
Which lives unchanged within, and his voice fell
Like music which makes giddy the dim brain,
Faint with intoxication of keen joy:
'Sister of her whose footsteps pave the world
With loveliness—more fair than aught but her,
Whose shadow thou art—lift thine eyes on me.'
I lifted them; the overpowering light
Of that immortal shape was shadowed o'er
By love; which, from his soft and flowing limbs,
And passion-parted lips, and keen, faint eyes,
Steamed forth like vaporous fire; an atmosphere
Which wrapped me in its all-dissolving power,
As the warm ether of the morning sun
Wraps ere it drinks some cloud of wandering dew.
I saw not, heard not, moved not, only felt
His presence flow and mingle through my blood
Till it became his life, and his grew mine,
And I was thus absorbed, until it passed,
And like the vapors when the sun sinks down,
Gathering again in drops upon the pines,
And tremulous as they, in the deep night
My being was condensed; and as thy rays
Of thought were slowly gathered, I could hear
His voice, whose accents lingered ere they died
Like footsteps of weak melody; thy name
Among the many sounds alone I heard
Of what might be articulate; though still
I listened through the night when sound was none.
Ione wakened then, and said to me:
'Canst thou divine what troubles me tonight?
I always knew what I desired before,
Nor ever found delight to wish in vain.
But now I cannot tell thee what I seek;
I know not; something sweet, since it is sweet
Even to desire; it is thy sport, false sister;
Thou hast discovered some enchantment old,

Whose spells have stolen my spirit as I slept
And mingled it with thine; for when just now
We kissed, I felt within thy parted lips
The sweet air that sustained me; and the warmth
Of the life-blood, for loss of which I faint,
Quivered between our intertwining arms.'
I answered not, for the Eastern star grew pale,
But fled to thee.

Romance

Edward Sheldon
1913

Scene: a society party

Serio-Comic
    Rita: a worldly young woman from Italy, 20s

Here, the passionate Rita tells the tale of her first love to Van Tuyl, an older man to whom she is very much attracted.

RITA (Ironically.): I never tol' you of my first so bee-eautiful romance? No—? Vell, I do not often t'ink of it—it make me feel—(*With a curious little shiver.*)—not nize. (*Pause.*) It vas in Venice. I vas jus' seexteen years ol'. I play de guitar wid de *serenata*—you know, the leetle company of peoples dat go about an' sing under de vindows of de great 'otels—(*With a sigh.*) *Ah, Madonna! come sembra lontano!*
[*VAN TUYL:* Well?]
RITA (Not looking at him.): A young man come join our serenata— Beppo, 'is name vas—Beppo Aquilone. 'E vas 'an'some an' 'e 'ad nize voice—oh, ver' light, you know, but steel—*simpatica.* Ve stan' to-gether vhen ve sing an' 'ave—I dunno—vone, two duet. An' so it go for two—t'ree veek an' 'e say noding much, but every time 'e smile an' look at me my 'eart is full vit' great beeg vishes an' I feel like everyt'ing in all de vorld is new an' born again. An' so vone evening 'e come vit' me to my leetle room—an' den 'e tell me dat 'e love me— an' all night long 'e 'old me close an' keess me— An' I feel 'is 'ot breat' like a fire upon my face—an' de beating of 'is 'eart, it come like strong blows 'ere against my own. An' den 'e sleep. But I—I do not sleep. I lie still an' qviet an' in my mind I have vone t'ought—"Is dis vhat people mean vhen dey say—love?" An' so de 'ours go by, an' de night is feenish, an' a—a—'ow you say?—a long, t'in piece of sun-light, it creep in my leetle vindow an' it shine on Beppo vhere 'e lie beside me. An' oh! 'e look so young!—an' den de sunlight—'ow you say?—it tease him, so 'e 'alf vake up, an' 'e vink 'is eyes an' say, "Ah, Rita, ti amo!" An den 'e sigh an' put 'is 'ead 'ere—on my shoulder— like a leetle baby dat is tired, an' go to sleep again. (*With passionate tenderness.*) An' oh! I put my arm about 'im an' I smile an' t'ink, "For

Love I vaited all night long, an' vit' de day—it come!"

[*VAN TUYL:* And so it does, my dear.]

RITA (*In a different voice.*): You t'ink so? Vait—! (*She has turned away.*) In tvelve 'our—*tvelve 'our!*—'e sell me to an English traveler for feefty *lire*. At first, I t'ink I die—I soffer so! An' den at las' I on'erstan'—an' laugh—an' know dat I 'ave been vone great beeg fool—

[*VAN TUYL* (*Protesting.*): My dear, I—]

RITA (*Shaking her clenched hands.*): A fool to t'ink dere vas some greater, better love—a love dat come at morning an' shine like sunshine—(*With a wide gesture.*)—yes, all t'rough de day!

[*VAN TUYL:* There is.]

RITA (*Fiercely.*): Dat is vone lie! You 'ear—? vone lie! (*Voluptuously.*) Love—it is made of keesses in de dark, of 'ot breat' on de face an' 'eart beats jus' like terrible strong blows! It is a struggle—ver' cruel and' sveet—all full of madness an' of vhispered vords an' leetle laughs dat turn into a sigh! Love is de 'unger for anoder's flesh—a deep down t'irst to dreenk anoder's blood— Love is a beast dat feed all t'rough de night an' vhen de morning come—*Love dies!* (*Slight pause.*)

The Ruddigore or
The Witch's Curse

William Schwenk Gilbert
1887

Scene: The fishing village of Rederring in Cornwall

Serio-Comic
> Rose Maybud: a village maiden of discriminating taste, 18–20

> When asked by her aunt why she has yet to accept a suitor, Rose reveals that she lives by very strict rules of etiquette, and may therefore never reveal her true feelings to a man.

ROSE: Hush, dear aunt, for thy words pain me sorely. Hung in a plated dish-cover to the knocker of the work-house door, with naught that I could call mine own, save a change of baby-linen and a book of etiquette, little wonder if I have always regarded that work as a voice from a parent's tomb. This hallowed volume (*Producing a book of etiquette.*), composed, if I may believe the title-page, by no less an authority than the wife of a Lord Mayor, has been, through life, my guide and monitor. By its solemn precepts I have learnt to test the moral worth of all who approach me. The man who bites his bread, or eats peas with a knife, I look upon as a lost creature, and he who has not acquired the proper way of entering and leaving a room is the object of my pitying horror. There are those in this village who bite their nails, dear aunt, and nearly all are wont to use their pocket combs in public places. In truth I could pursue this painful theme much further, but behold, I have said enough.

Salomé

Oscar Wilde
1891

Scene: the court of Herod

Dramatic
> Salomé: headstrong daughter of Herodias, 16–18

> Salomé has danced for Herod for which she receives the head of John the Baptist.
> Here, she addresses her grief to the prophet's severed head.

SALOMÉ: Ah! thou wouldst not suffer me to kiss thy mouth, Jokanaan. Well, I will kiss it now. I will bite it with my teeth as one bites a ripe fruit. Yes, I will kiss thy mouth, Jokanaan. I said it; did I not say it? I said it. Ah! I will kiss it now. . . . But, wherefore dost thou not look at me, Jokanaan? Thine eyes that were so terrible, so full of rage and scorn, are shut now. Wherefore are they shut? Open thine eyes! Lift up thine eyelids, Jokanaan! Wherefore dost thou not look at me? Art thou afraid of me, Jokanaan, that thou wilt not look at me? . . . And thy tongue, that was like a red snake darting poison, it moves no more, it speaks no words, Jokanaan, that scarlet viper that spat its venom upon me. It is strange, is it not? How is it that the red viper stirs no longer? . . . Thou wouldst have none of me, Jokanaan. Thou rejectedst me. Thou didst speak evil words against me. Thou didst bear thyself toward me as to a harlot, as to a woman that is a wanton, to me, Salomé, daughter of Herodias, Princess of Judæa! Well, I still live, but thou art dead, and thy head belongs to me. I can do with it what I will. I can throw it to the dogs and to the birds of the air. That which the dogs leave, the birds of the air shall devour. . . . Ah, Jokanaan, thou wert the man that I loved alone among men. All other men were hateful to me. But thou wert beautiful! Thy body was a column of ivory set upon feet of silver. It was a garden full of doves and lilies of silver. It was a tower of silver decked with shields of ivory. There was nothing in the world so white as thy body. There was nothing in the world so black as thy hair. In the whole world there was nothing so red as thy mouth. Thy voice was a censer that scattered strange perfumes, and when I looked on thee I heard a strange music. Ah! wherefore didst thou not look at me, Jokanaan? With the cloak of thine hands and with the cloak of thy blasphemies thou didst hide thy face. Thou didst put upon thine eyes the covering of him who would see his God. Well, thou hast seen thy God, Jokanaan, but me, me, thou didst never see. If thou hadst seen me thou hadst loved me. I saw thee, and I loved thee. Oh, how I loved thee! I love thee yet, Jokanaan, I love only thee. . . . I am athirst for thy beauty; I am hungry for thy body; and neither wine nor apples can appease my desire. What shall I do now, Jokanaan? Neither the floods nor the great waters can quench my passion. I was a princess, and thou didst scorn me. I was a virgin, and thou didst take my virginity from me. I was chaste, and thou didst fill my veins with fire. . . . Ah! ah! wherefore didst thou not look at me? If thou hadst looked at me thou hadst loved me. Well I know that thou wouldst have loved me, and the mystery of love is greater than the mystery of death.

The Second Mrs. Tanqueray

Arthur Wing Pinero
1893

Scene: England

#1—Dramatic
  Paula: a woman chafing in her life as the wife of a country lord, 30s

  Paula longed to marry Aubrey Tanqueray in order to improve her place in society. She was unprepared, however, for the tedium of life on a country estate. The
  endless succession of days have made her quite stir-crazy as she here reveals to
  Aubrey.

PAULA: Oh! I've no patience with you! You'll kill me with this life!
(*She selects some flowers from a vase on the table, cuts and arranges them,
and fastens them in her bodice.*) What is my existence, Sunday to Satur-
day? In the morning, a drive down to the village, with the groom, to
give my orders to the tradespeople. At lunch, you and Ellean. In the
afternoon, a novel, the newspapers: if fine, another drive—*if fine!*
Tea—you and Ellean. Then two hours of dusk; then dinner—you and
Ellean. Then a game of Bésique, you and I, while Ellean reads a reli-
gious book, in a dull corner. Then a yawn from me, another from
you, a sigh from Ellean; three figures suddenly rise—"Good-night,
good-night, good-night!" (*Imitating a kiss.*) "God bless you!" Ah!
[*AUBREY:* Yes, yes, Paula—yes, dearest—that's what it is now. But,
by-and-by, if people begin to come round us—]
PAULA: Hah! That's where we've made the mistake, my friend
Aubrey! (*Pointing to the window.*) Do you believe these people will
ever come round us? Your former crony, Mrs. Cortelyon? Or the grim
old vicar, or that wife of his whose huge nose is positively indecent?
Or the Ullathornes, or the Gollans, or Lady William Petres? I know
better! And when the young ones gradually take the place of the old,
there will still remain the sacred tradition that the dreadful person
who lives at the top of the hill is never, under any circumstances, to
be called upon! And so we shall go on here, year in and year out,
until the sap is run out of our lives, and we're stale and dry and withered from sheer, solitary respectability. Upon my word, I wonder we
didn't see that we should have been far happier if we'd gone in for
the devil-may-care, *café*-living sort of life in town! After all, *I* have a

set, and you might have joined it. It's true, I did want, dearly, dearly, to be a married woman, but where's the pride in being a married woman among married women who are—married! If—(*Seeing that Aubrey's head has sunk into his hands*.) Aubrey! My dear boy! You're not—crying?

#2—Dramatic
    Paula

Here, Paula confronts Ellean, Aubrey's daughter from his first marriage, and begs the young woman to accept her as her new mother.

PAULA: Dreams are only a hash-up of one's day-thoughts, I suppose you know. Think intently of anything, and it's bound to come back to you at night. I don't cultivate dreams myself.
[ELLEAN: Ah, I knew you would only sneer!]
PAULA: I'm not sneering; I'm speaking the truth. I say that if you cared for me in the daytime I should soon make friends with those nightmares of yours. Ellean, why don't you try to look on me as your second mother? Of course there are not many years between us, but I'm ever so much older than you—in experience. I shall have no children of my own, I know that; it would be a real comfort to me if you would make me feel we belonged to each other. Won't you? Perhaps you think I'm odd—not nice. Well, the fact is I've two sides to my nature, and I've let the one almost smother the other. A few years ago I went through some trouble, and since then I haven't shed a tear. I believe if you put your arms around me just once I should run upstairs and have a good cry. There, I've talked to you as I've never talked to a woman in my life. Ellean, you seem to fear me. Don't! Kiss me!

#3—Dramatic
    Paula

Paula's constant anxiety over life minutiae has finally caused her marriage to fail. Aubrey suggests that they travel abroad and try to begin again. It is too late, however, for Paula's descent into madness is complete. Here, she rejects Aubrey's notion of a better future and darkly alludes to her plan to commit suicide.

PAULA: I believe the future is only the past again, entered though another gate.
[AUBREY: That's an awful belief.]

PAULA: To-night proves it. You must see now that, do what we will, go where we will, you'll be continually reminded of—what I was. I see it.

[AUBREY: You're frightened to-night; meeting this man has frightened you. But that sort of thing isn't likely to recur. The world isn't quite so small as all that.]

PAULA: Isn't it? The only great distances it contains are those we carry within ourselves—the distances that separate husbands and wives, for instance. And so it'll be with us. You'll do your best—oh, I know that—you're a good fellow. But circumstances will be too strong for you in the end, mark my words.

[AUBREY: Paula—!]

PAULA: Of course I'm pretty now—I'm pretty still—and a pretty woman, whatever else she may be, is always—well, endurable. But even now I notice that the lines of my face are getting deeper; so are the hollows about my eyes. Yes, my face is covered with little shadows that usen't to be there. Oh, I know I'm "going off." I hate paint and dye and those messes, but, by-and-by, I shall drift the way of the others; I sha'n't be able to help myself. And then, some day—perhaps very suddenly, under a queer, fantastic light at night or in the glare of the morning—that horrid, irresistible truth that physical repulsion forces on men and women will come to you, and you'll sicken at me.

[AUBREY: I—!]

PAULA: You'll see then, at last, with other people's eyes you'll see me just as your daughter does now, as all wholesome folks see women like me. And I shall have no weapon to fight with—not one serviceable little bit of prettiness left me to defend myself with! A worn-out creature—broken up, very likely, some time before I ought to be—my hair bright, my eyes dull, my body too thin or too stout, my cheeks raddled and ruddled—a ghost, a wreck, a caricature, a candle that gutters, call such an end what you like! Oh, Aubrey, what shall I be able to say to you then? And this is the future you talk about! I know it—I know it! (*He is still sitting staring forward; she rocks herself to and fro as if in pain.*) Oh, Aubrey! Oh! Oh!

The Ticket-of-Leave Man

Tom Taylor
1863

Scene: London

#1—Dramatic
        May: a woman in dire straits, 20s

> May's husband has been sent to prison, leaving her with no money. Here, the
> destitute woman reads a recent letter from him aloud to her canary.

MAY: There, Goldie, I must give *you* your breakfast, though I don't
care a bit for my own. Ah! you find singing a better trade than I did,
you little rogue. I'm sure I shall have a letter from Robert this morning. I've all his letters here. (*Taking out a packet from her work-box.*)
How he has improved in his handwriting since the first. (*Opening letter.*) That's more than three years back. Oh! what an old woman I'm
getting! It's no use denying it, Goldie. (*To her bird.*) If you'll be quiet,
like a good, well-bred canary, I'll read you Robert's last letter.
(*Reads.*) "Portland, February 25th, 1860. My own dearest May,—(*Kissing it.*) As the last year keeps slipping away, I think more and more of
our happy meeting; but for your love and comfort I think I should
have broken down." Goldie, do you hear that? (*She kisses the letter.*)
"But now we both see how things are guided for the best. But for my
being sent to prison, I should have died before this, a broken-down
drunkard, if not worse; and you might still have been earning hard
bread as a street-singer, or carried from a hospital ward to a pauper's
grave." Yes, yes, (*Shuddering.*) that's true. "This place has made a
man of me, and you have found friends and the means of earning a
livelihood. I count the days till we meet. Good-bye and heaven bless
you, prays your ever affectionate Robert Brierly." (*Kisses the letter fre-
quently.*) And don't I count the days too? There! (*Makes a mark in her
pocket almanack.*) Another gone! They seem so slow—when one looks
forward—and yet they pass so quickly! (*Taking up birdcage.*) Come,
Goldie, while I work you must sing me a nice song for letting you
hear that nice letter.

Mrs. Willoughby: May's landlady, 40–50

Here, May is paid a visit by her talkative landlady, whose favorite topic of conversation seems to be herself.

MRS. WILLOUGHBY: You'll excuse me if I take a chair, (Sits, L.) these stairs is trying to an elderly woman—not that I am so old as many that looks younger, which when I'd my front tittivated only last week, Mr. Miggles, that's the hairdresser at 22, he says to me, "Mrs. Willoughby," he says, "forty is what I'd give you with that front," he says. "No, Mr. Miggles," I says, "forty it was once, but will never be again, which trouble is a sharp thorn, and losses is more than time, and a shortness of breath along of a shock three years was last July." "No, Mr. Miggles," I says, "fronts can't undo the work of years," I says, "nor yet wigs, Mr. Miggles—which skin-partings equal to years, I never did see, and that's the truth." (Pauses for breath.)
[MAY: At all events, Mrs. Willoughby, you're looking very, very well this morning.]
MRS. WILLOUGHBY: Ah, my dear, you are very good to say so, which, if it wasn't for rheumatics and the rates, one atop of another, and them dustmen, which their carts is a mockery, unless you stand beer, and that boy, Sam, though which is the worst, I'm sure is hard to say, only a grandmother's feelings is not to be told, which opodeldoc can't be rubbed into the 'eart, as I said to Mrs. Molloy—her that has my first floor front—which she says to me, "Mrs. Willoughby," says she, "nine oils is the thing," she says, "rubbed in warm," says she. "Which it's all very well, Mrs. Molloy," says I, "but how is a lone woman to rub it in the nape of the neck and the small of the back; and Sam that giddy, and distressing me to that degree. No, Mrs. Molloy," I says, "what's sent us we must bear it, and parties that's reduced to let lodgings, can't afford easy chairs," which well I know it, and the truth it is—and me with two beauties in chintz in the front parlour, which I got a bargain at the brokers when the parties was sold up at 24, and no more time to sit down in 'em than if I was a cherrybin.

Uncle Vanya

Anton Chekhov, tr. by Stark Young
1899

Scene: a country estate in Russia

Dramatic
>   Sonya: a woman rejected by the man she loves, 20–30

>   Sonya realizes that there is no marriage in her future and that she will live out her
>   days as a spinster on her father's country estate. Here, she commiserates with
>   Uncle Vanya, who shares a similar fate.

SONYA: But what can we do, Uncle? We're alive. (*A pause.*) We'll
live, through a long chain of days, endless nights. We'll bear pa-
tiently whatever happens; we'll work for others, until we die, with no
rest, and when our hour has come we'll go without a murmur. But in
the next world, Uncle, we'll say that we suffered, that we were miserable, and God will have pity on us. Then, dear Uncle, a new life will
start—radiant, beautiful; we'll rejoice and we'll remember these sufferings with a smile; we'll rest. I believe that, Uncle, with all my
heart. (*She kneels in front of him and puts her hand on her uncle's hands.
She speaks in a tired voice.*) We'll rest. (*Tyelyegyin quietly plays the
guitar.*) Yes, rest! We'll hear the angels sing, thy sky will be filled with
diamonds. All our trouble and pain will melt, there'll be compassion.
Our lives will be calm and gentle, sweet as a caress. . . . I believe that,
Uncle, I believe it. (*With her handkerchief she wipes away her uncle's
tears.*) Dear, poor Uncle Vanya, you're crying. (*Through her own tears.*)
You've had no joy in your life, but wait, Uncle, just wait. . . . We'll rest.
. . . (*She embraces him.*) We'll rest. (*We hear the tapping of the night
watchman. Tyelyegyin plays softly. Mariya Vasilyevna writes in the mar-
gins of her pamphlet. Maryina knits a stocking.*) We'll rest.

Vera or The Nilhilists

Oscar Wilde
1880

Setting: Moscow, 1800

Dramatic
   Vera: The outspoken daughter of an innkeeper, 20s

   When the Czar declares martial law, Vera speaks passionately in favor of revolution.

VERA: Martial law! O God, how easy it is for a king to kill his people by thousands, but we cannot rid ourselves of one crowned man in Europe! What is there of awful majesty in these men which makes the hand unsteady, the dagger treacherous, the pistol-shot harmless? Are they not men of like passions with ourselves, vulnerable to the same diseases, of flesh and blood not different from our own? What made Olgiati tremble at the supreme crisis of that Roman life, and Guido's nerve fail him when he should have been of iron and of steel? A plague, I say, on these fools of Naples, Berlin, and Spain! Methinks that if I stood face to face with one of the crowned men my eye would see more clearly, my aim be more sure, my whole body gain a strength and power that was not my own! Oh, to think what stands between us and freedom in Europe! a few old men wrinkled, feeble, tottering dotards whom a boy could strangle for a ducat, or a woman stab in a night-time. And these are the things that keep us from democracy, that keep us from liberty. But now methinks the brood of men is dead and the dull earth grown sick of childbearing, else would no crowned dog pollute God's air by living.

Widowers' Houses

George Bernard Shaw
1892

Setting: London

Serio-Comic
Blanche: a young woman furious with her fiancé, 18–20

Blanche has rashly broken off her engagement to Harry, with whom she is still very much in love. Several months later, Harry visits Blanche and she greets him with anger which soon melts into affection.

BLANCHE (*Shrewishly.*): Well? So you have come back here. You have had the meanness to come into this house again. (*He flushes and retreats a step. She follows him up remorselessly.*) What a poor spirited creature you must be! Why don't you go? (*Red and wincing, he starts huffily to get his hat from the table; but when he turns to the door with it she deliberately stands in his way; so that he has to stop.*) I don't want you to stay. (*For a moment, they stand face to face, quite close to one another, she provocative, taunting, half defying, half inviting to advance, in a flush of undisguised animal excitement. It suddenly flashes on him that all this ferocity is erotic; that she is making love to him. His eye lights up: a cunning expression comes into the corners of his mouth: with a heavy assumption of indifference he walks straight back to his chair, and plants himself in it with his arms folded. She comes down the room after him.*) But I forgot: you have found that there is some money to be made here. Lickcheese told you. You, who were so disinterested, so independent, that you could not accept anything from my father! (*At the end of every sentence she waits to see what execution she has done.*) I suppose you will try to persuade me that you have come down here on a great philanthropic enterprise—to befriend the poor by having those houses rebuilt, eh? (*Trench maintains his attitude and makes no sign.*) Yes: when my father makes you do it. And when Lickcheese has discovered some way of making it profitable. Oh, I know papa; and I know you. And for the sake of that, you come back here—into the house where you were refused—ordered out. (*Trench's face darkens: her eyes gleam as she sees it.*) Aha! you remember that. You know it's true: you can't deny it. (*She sits down and softens her tone a little as she affects to pity him.*) Well, let

84

me tell you that you cut a poor figure, a very, very poor figure, Harry. (*At the word Harry he relaxes the fold of his arms; and a faint grin of anticipated victory appears on his face.*) And you, too, a gentleman! so highly connected! with such distinguished relations! so particular as to where your money comes from! I wonder at you. I really wonder at you. I should have thought that if your fine family gave you nothing else, it might at least have given you some sense of personal dignity. Perhaps you think you look dignified at present: eh? (*No reply.*) Well, I can assure you that you don't: you look most ridiculous—as foolish as a man could look—you don't know what to do. But after all, I really don't see what any one could say in defence of such conduct. (*He looks straight in front of him, and purses up his lips as if whistling. This annoys her; and she becomes affectedly polite.*) I am afraid I am in your way, Dr. Trench. (*She rises.*) I shall not intrude on you any longer. You seem so perfectly at home that I need make no apology for leaving you to yourself. (*She makes a feint of going to the door; but he does not budge; and she returns and comes behind his chair.*) Harry. (*He does not turn. She comes a stop nearer.*) Harry: I want you to answer me a question. (*Earnestly, stooping over him.*) Look me in the face. (*No reply.*) Do you hear? (*Seizing his cheeks and twisting his head round.*) Look—me—in—the—face. (*He shuts his eyes tight and grins. She suddenly kneels down beside him with her breast against his shoulder.*) Harry: what were you doing with my photograph just now, when you thought you were alone?

Men's Monologues

André

William Dunlop
1798

Scene: The village of Tappan, NY during the Revolutionary War

#1—Dramatic
> Melville: a Captain in the Colonial army, 40s

> Melville is standing the night watch at an encampment outside of Tappan. Here, he takes a moment to reflect on the dark nature of war.

MELVILLE: The solemn hour, "when night and morning meet."
Mysterious time, to superstition dear,
And superstition's guides, now passes by;
Deathlike in solitude. The sentinels,
In drowsy tones, from post to post send on
The signal of the passing hour. "All's well,"
Sounds through the camp. Alas, all is not well;
Else, why stand I, as man, the friend of man,
At midnight's depth, deck'd in this murderous guise,
The habiliment of death, the badge of dire
Necessitous coercion. 'Tis not well.
—In vain the enlighten'd friends of suffering man
Point out, of war, the folly, guilt, and madness.
Still, age succeeds to age, and war to war;
And man, the murderer, marshals out in hosts
In all gaiety of festive pomp,
To spread around him death and desolation.
How long! how long!—
—Methinks I hear the tread of feet this way.
My meditating mood may work me woe.
(*Draws.*) Stand, whoso'er thou art. Answer.
Who's there?

Major André: a captured British officer, 20-30

On the last night of his life, this convicted British spy contemplates his impending death

ANDRÉ: Kind Heaven be thank'd for that I stand alone
In this sad hour of life's brief pilgrimage!
Single in misery; no one else involving.
In grief, in shame, and ruin. 'T is my comfort.
Thou, my thrice honor'd sire, in peace went'st down
Unto the tomb, nor knew to blush, not knew
A pang for me. And thou, revered matron,
Could'st bless thy child, and yield thy breath in peace!
No wife shall weep, no child lament my loss.
Thus may I consolation find in what
Was once my woe. I little thought to joy
In not possessing, as I erst possest,
thy love, Honora! André's death, perhaps,
May cause a cloud pass o'er thy lovely face;
The pearly tear may steal from either eye;
For thou mayest feel a transient pang, nor wrong
A husband's rights: more than a transient pang
O mayest thou never feel! The morn draws nigh
To light me to my shame. Frail nature shrinks—
And *is* death then so fearful? I have brav'd
Him, fearless, in the field, and steel'd my breast
Against his thousand horrors; but his cool,
His sure approach, requires a fortitude
Which naught but conscious rectitude can give.

Arms and the Man

George Bernard Shaw
1894

Scene: Bulgaria, 1885

Serio-Comic
Nicola: a devoted servant, 30–40

Nicola takes his position in the Petkoff household very seriously. When Louka, a peasant-girl-turned-chambermaid, behaves in a manner he believes to be above her station, he lectures her on the importance of knowing one's place.

NICOLA (*Turning, still on his knees, and squatting down rather forlornly on his calves, daunted by her implacable disdain.*): You have a great ambition in you, Louka. Remember: if any luck comes to you, it was I that made a woman of you.

[*LOUKA*: You!]

NICOLA (*Scrambling up and going at her.*): Yes, me. Who was it made you give up wearing a couple of pounds of false black hair on your head and reddening your lips and cheeks like any other Bulgarian girl? I did. Who taught you to trim your nails, and keep your hands clean, and be dainty about yourself, like a fine Russian lady? Me: do you hear that? me! (*She tosses her head defiantly; and he turns away, adding, more coolly.*) I've often thought that if Raina were out of the way, and you just a little less of a fool and Sergius just a little more of one, you might come to be one of my grandest customers, instead of only being my wife and costing me money.

[*LOUKA*: I believe you would rather be my servant than my husband. You would make more out of me. Oh, I know that soul of yours.]

NICOLA (*Going closer to her for greater emphasis.*): Never you mind my soul; but just listen to my advice. If you want to be a lady, your present behavior to me won't do at all, unless when we're alone. It's too sharp and impudent; and impudence is a sort of familiarity: it shews affection for me. And don't you try being high and mighty with me, either. You're like all country girls: you think it's genteel to treat a servant the way I treat a stableboy. That's only your ignorance; and don't you forget it. And don't be so ready to defy everybody. Act as if you expected to have your own way, not as if you expected to be ordered about. The way to get on as a lady is the same as the way to get on as a servant: you've got to know your place: that's the secret of it. And you may depend on me to know my place if you get promoted. Think over it my girl. I'll stand by you; one servant should always stand by another.

Bertram or
The Castle of St. Aldobrand

Charles Robert Maturin
1816

Scene: England

Dramatic

Bertram: a man plotting revenge, 30s

After wandering the land as a bandit for several years, Bertram has finally returned home to the woman he loves, only to discover that she has married his rival. Here, he roams the forest at night and considers his revenge.

BERTRAM: Was he a man fiend?—Whate'er it was
It hath dealt wonderfully with me—
All is around his dwelling suitable;
The invisible blast to which the dark pines grown,
The unconscious tread to which the thick earth echoes,
The hidden waters rushing to their fall,
These sounds of which the causes are not seen
I love, for they are like my fate mysterious—
How tower'd his proud form through the shrouding gloom,
How spoke the eloquent silence of its motion,
How through the barred vizor did his accents
Roll their rich thunder on their[1] pausing soul!
And though his mailed hand did shun my grasp,
And though his closed morion hid his feature,
Yea all resemblance to the face of man,
I felt the hollow whisper of his welcome,
I felt those unseen eyes were fix'd on mine,
If eyes indeed were there—
Forgotten thoughts of evil, still-born mischiefs,
Foul, fertile seeds of passion and of crime,
The night-veiled thoughts of many a ghastly hour
Day may not look upon—
That wither'd in my heart's abortive core,

---

[1]For "the"?

Rous'd their dark battle at his trumpet-peal:
So sweeps the tempest o'er the slumbering desert,
Waking its myriad hosts of burning death:
So calls the last dread peal the wandering atoms
Of bone and blood, rent flesh and dust-worn fragments,
In dire array of ghastly unity,
To bide the eternal summons—
I am not what I was since I beheld him—
I was the slave of passion's ebbing sway—
All is condensed, collected, callous now—
The groan, the burst, the fiery flash is o'er,
Down pours the dense and darkening lava-tide,
Arresting life and stilling all beneath it.

Black-ey'd Susan

Douglas Jerrold
1829

Scene: the harbor

#1—Dramatic
   William: a sailor, 30s

   After many months at sea, William finally returns home, his thoughts on one person only: his lovely wife Susan.

WILLIAM: Avast there! hang it—that name, spoke by another, has brought the salt water up; I can feel one tear standing in either eye like a marine at each gangway: but come, let's send them below. (*Wipes his eyes.*) Now, don't pay away your line till I pipe. I have been three years at sea; all that time I heard but once from Susan—she has been to me a main-stay in all weathers. I have been piped up— roused from my hammock, dreaming of her—for the cold black middle watch; I have walked the deck, the surf beating in my face, but Susan was at my side, and I did not feel it; I have been reefing on the yards, in cold and darkness, when I could hardly see the hand of my next messmate—but Susan's eyes were on me, and there was light; I have heard the boatswain pipe to quarters—a voice in my heart whispered "Susan!" it was a word that seemed to turn the balls aside, and keep me safe. When land was cried from the mast head, I seized the glass—my shipmates saw the cliffs of England—I, I could see but Susan! I leap upon the beach; my shipmates find hands to grasp and lips to press—I find not Susan's.

#2—Serio-Comic
   William

   Here, William spins a dark yarn about St. Domingo Billy, a man-eating shark he encountered in the Caribbean.

WILLIAM: It's lucky for you, that you've been good to Susan, or I shouldn't spin you these yarns. You see it was when the fleet was lying off St. Domingo, in the West Indies, the crew like new rum and dancing with the niggers; well, the Admiral, (a good old fellow, and one as didn't like flogging), wouldn't give the men liberty; some of 'em, howsomever, would swim ashore at night, and come off in the morning. Now, you see, to hinder this, the Admiral and the Captains put St. Domingo Billy on the ship's books, and served him out his mess every morning.

[*GNATBRAIN:* Who was St. Domingo Billy?]

WILLIAM: Why, a shark, as long as the Captain's gig. This shark, or Billy, for that's what the sailors called him, used to swim round the fleet, and go from ship to ship, for his biscuit and raw junk, just like a Christian.

[*GNATBRAIN:* Well, but your 'bacco-box, what about that?]

WILLIAM: Steady! I'm coming to it. Well, one morning, about eight bells, there was a black bumboat woman aboard, with a little piccaninny, not much longer than my hand; well, she sat just in the gangway, and there was Billy along side, with his three decks of grinders, ready for what might come,—well, afore you could say aboutship, the little black baby jumped out of its mothers grappling, and fell into Billy's jaws,—the black woman gave a shriek that would have split the boatswain's whistle! Tom Gunnel saw how the wind was: he was as fine a seaman as ever stept—stood six feet two, and could sit upon his pig-tail. Well, he snatched up a knife, overboard he jumps, dives under Billy, and in a minute the sea was as red as a marine; all the crew hung like a swarm of bees upon the shrouds, and when Tom came up, all over blood with the corpse of the baby in his hand, and the shark turned over dead upon its side—my eyes! such a cheer—it might have been heard at Greenwich. We had 'em aboard, cut up Billy, and what do you think we found in him? All the watches and 'bacco-boxes as had been lost for the last ten years—an Admiral's cocked hat, and three pilots' telescopes. This is one on 'em!

The Castle Spectre

Matthew G. Lewis
1797

Scene: England

Dramatic

Reginald: a man held captive by his evil brother, 50s

Reginald has been kept in a dungeon by his scheming brother for many years. Here, he paces this lonely cell and longs for freedom.

REGINALD: My child! My Evelina!—Oh! fly me not, lovely forms!— They are gone, and once more I live to misery.—Thou wert kind to me, Sleep!—Even now, methought, "I sat in my Castle-hall:—" A maid, lovely as the Queen of Fairies, hung on my knee, and hailed me by that sweet name, "Father!"—"Yes, I was happy!—Yet frown not on me therefore, Darkness!—I am thine again, my gloomy bride!—Be not incensed, Despair, that I left thee for a moment; I have passed with thee sixteen years!—Ah! how many have I still to pass?—Yet fly not my bosom quite, sweet Hope!—Still speak to me of liberty, of light!—Whisper, that once more I shall see the morn break—that again shall my fevered lips drink the pure gale of evening!" —God, thou know'st that I have borne my sufferings meekly; I have wept for myself, but never cursed my foes; I have sorrowed for thy anger, but never murmured at thy will.—"Patient have I been—Oh! then reward me!"—Let me once again[2] press my daughter in my arms!—Let me, for one instant, feel again that I clasp to my heart a being that loves me!—Speed thou to heaven, prayer of a captive!— (*He sinks upon a stone, with his hands, clasped, and his eyes bent stedfastly upon the flame of the lamp.*)

[2]The Larpent version has "Let me then once."

The Cenci

Percy Bysshe Shelley
1820

Scene: 16th Century Rome

Dramatic

Count Francesco Cenci: a powerful and evil man, 50s

Count Cenci has come to wield great power in Rome. Here, he reveals the delight he takes in the suffering of others.

CENCI: Why miserable?—
No. I am what your theologians call
Hardened; which they must be in impudence,
So to revile a man's peculiar taste.
True, I was happier than I am, while yet
Manhood remained to act the thing I thought;
While lust was sweeter than revenge; and now
Invention palls: ay, we must all grow old:
And but that there yet remains a deed to act
Whose horror might make sharp an appetite
Duller than mine—I'd do,—I know not what.
When I was young I thought of nothing else
But pleasure; and I fed on honey sweets:
Men, by St. Thomas! cannot live like bees,
And I grew tired: yet, till I killed a foe,
And heard his groans, and heard his children's groans,
Knew I not what delight was else on earth,
Which now delights me little. I the rather
Look on such pangs as terror ill conceals:
The dry, fixed eyeball; the pale, quivering lip,
Which tell me that the spirit weeps within
Tears bitterer than the bloody sweat of Christ.
I rarely kill the body, which preserves,
Like a strong prison, the soul within my power,
Wherein I feel it with the breath of fear
For hourly pain.

Danton's Death

Georg Buchner, tr. by Henry J. Schmidt
1835

Scene: Paris during the Reign of Terror

#1—Dramatic
 Robespierre: architect of the Reign of Terror, 30–40

At a meeting of the National Committee, Robespierre speaks out in defense of the use of violence.

ROBESPIERRE: I wish to speak.

[THE JACOBINS: Listen! Listen to the Incorruptible!]

ROBESPIERRE: We were waiting only for the cry of discontent to ring out from all sides before we speak. Our eyes were open, we watched the enemy arming himself and rising up, but we did not sound the alarm. We let the people be their own guard; they have not slept, they have taken up arms. We let the enemy emerge from his cover, we let him advance; now he stands exposed in broad daylight, every blow will strike him, he is dead as soon as you have caught sight of him.

I have told you once before that the internal enemies of the Republic are split into two factions, like two armies. Under banners of various colors and on quite different paths they all rush toward the same goal. One of these factions no longer exists.[3] In its presumptuous madness it tried to cast aside the most proven patriots, branding them worn-out weaklings in order to rob the Republic of its strongest arms. It declared war on the Deity and on property in order to create a diversion on behalf of the kings. It parodied the exalted drama of the Revolution in order to compromise it through premeditated excesses. Hébert's triumph would have turned the Republic into chaos, and despotism would have been satisfied. The sword of judgment has struck the traitor down. But what does it matter to our foreign enemies when criminals of another sort remain to accomplish the same purpose? We have achieved nothing so long as another faction remains to be destroyed.

[3]The Hébertists.

This one is the opposite of the first. It leads us to weakness; its battle cry is: mercy! It intends to rob the people of their weapons and of their strength to fight in order to deliver them up to the kings, naked and unnerved.

The weapon of the Republic is terror, the strength of the Republic is virtue. Virtue: for without it, terror is corruptible; terror: for without it, virtue is powerless. Terror is an outgrowth of virtue; it is nothing more than swift, rigorous, and inflexible justice. Some say terror is the weapon of a despotic government, therefore ours resembles despotism. True, but in the way a sword in the hand of a hero of liberty resembles a saber in the hand of a tyrant's minion. If a tyrant rules his brutish subjects through terror, that is his right as a despot; if you destroy through terror the enemies of liberty, you, the founders of the Republic, are no less right. The Revolutionary government is the despotism of liberty against tyranny.

Mercy to the royalists! certain people cry. Mercy to the wicked? No! Mercy to the innocent, mercy to the weak, mercy to the unfortunate, mercy to humanity! Only the peaceful citizen deserves the protection of society. In a republic only republicans are citizens, royalists and foreigners are enemies. To punish the oppressors of mankind is charity, to pardon them is barbarity. I regard all traces of false sentimentality as sighs that fly to England or Austria.

Yet not content to disarm the people, some try to poison the most sacred sources of its strength through vice. This is the most subtle, most dangerous, and most deplorable attack against liberty. Vice is the mark of Cain on the aristocracy. Within a republic it is not only amoral but a political crime; the vice-ridden are the political enemies of liberty; the more they seem to accomplish in its service, the more dangerous they are. The most dangerous citizen is the one who wears out a dozen red caps more easily than doing one good deed.

You will understand me readily when you think about those who used to live in a garret and now ride in a carriage and fornicate with former marchionesses and baronesses. We may well ask: have the people been robbed or have we grasped the golden hands of the kings when we, the people's lawmakers, display all the vices and luxuries of former courtiers, when we see these marquises and barons of the Revolution marrying rich wives, giving sumptuous banquets, gambling, keeping servants and wearing expensive clothes? We may well be surprised when we hear them being witty, playing the snob, and adopting elegant manners. Lately someone shamelessly parodied Tacitus—I could answer like Sallust, and travesty Catiline; but no more brushstrokes are necessary, the portraits are complete.

Let there be no compromise, no truce with those who were only set on robbing the people, who hoped to rob them unpunished, for whom the Republic was business speculation and the Revolution a trade. Frightened by the rushing torrent of the examples we have set, they now very quietly seek to cool down our justice. We are to believe that they say to themselves: "We are not virtuous enough to be so terrible. Philosophic lawmakers, have mercy on our weakness! I don't dare to tell you that I am so wicked, so I'd rather tell you, don't be inhuman!"

Calm yourselves, virtuous people, calm yourselves, patriots: tell your brothers in Lyons that the sword of justice will not rust in the hands of those to whom you have entrusted it.—We will set a great example for the Republic.

#2—Dramatic
    Camille: a member of the National Committee, 40–50

    Here, the sardonic Camille bemoans the fact that art generally goes unappreciated by the masses.

CAMILLE: I tell you, if they aren't given everything in wooden copies, scattered about in theaters, concerts, and art exhibits, they'll have neither eyes nor ears for it. Let someone whittle a marionette where the strings pulling it are plainly visible and whose joints crack at every step in iambic pentameter: what a character, what consistency! Let someone take a little bit of feeling, an aphorism, a concept, and clothe it in a coat and pants, give it hands and feet, color its face and let the thing torment itself through three acts until it finally marries or shoots itself: an idea! Let someone fiddle an opera which reflects the rising and sinking of the human spirit the way a clay pipe with water imitates a nightingale: oh, art!

Take people out of the theater and put them in the street: oh, miserable reality! They forget their Creator because of His poor imitators. They see and hear nothing of Creation, which renews itself every moment in and around them, glowing, rushing, luminous. They go to the theater, read poetry and novels, make faces like the masks they find there, and say to God's creatures: how ordinary! The Greeks knew what they were saying when they declared that Pygmalion's statue did indeed come to life but never had any children.

Darnley

Edward Bulwer-Lytton
1877

Scene: London

Dramatic

Darnley: a harried husband, 30–40

When Darnley's foolish wife requests that they separate, he takes a moment to verbally vent his frustration with the fairer sex.

DARNLEY: Oh! let man beware of marriage until he thoroughly know the mind of her on whom his future must depend. Woe to him, agony and woe, when the wife feels no sympathy with the toil, when she soothes not in the struggle, when her heart is far from that world within, to which her breath gives the life, and her presence is the sun! How many men in humbler life have fled, from a cheerless hearth, to the haunts of guilt! How many in the convict's exile, in the felon's cell, might have shunned the fall—if woman (whom Heaven meant for our better angel) had allured their step from the first paths to hell by making a paradise of home! But by the poor the holy household ties are at least not scorned and trifled with, as by those among whom you were reared. *They* at least do not deem it a mean ambition that contents itself with the duties of wife and mother. Look round the gay world you live in, and when you see the faithless husband wasting health, fortune, honor, in unseemly vices—behold too often the cause of all in the cold eyes and barren heart of the fashionable wife.

De Montfort

Joanna Baillie
1800

Scene: a village in Germany

Dramatic

De Montfort: a man living in wretched turmoil, 20–30

De Montfort has spent the better part of his life hating his childhood rival, Rezen-velt. Indeed, this hatred has driven him away from his home and loved ones. Jane, his loving sister, has followed De Montfort, determined to bring him back, but when a stranger informs De Montfort that Rezenvelt intends to marry Jane, he falls into a murderous rage.

DE MONTFORT (*Comes forward to the front of the stage, and makes a long pause, expressive of great agony of mind.*):
It must be so; each passing circumstance;
Her hasty journey here; her keen distress
Whene'er my soul's abhorrence I express'd;
Ay, and that damned reconciliation,
With tears extorted from me: Oh, too well!
All, all too well bespeak the shameful tale.
I should have thought of heav'n and hell conjoin'd,
The morning star mix'd with infernal fire,
Ere I had thought of this—[4]
"Hell's blackest magick, in the midnight hour,
"With horrid spells and incantation dire,
"Such combination opposite, unseemly,
"Of fair and loathsome, excellent and base,
"Did ne'er produce.—But every thing is possible,
"So as it may my misery enhance!"
Oh! I did love her with such pride of soul!
When other men, in gayest pursuit of love,
Each beauty follow'd, by her side I stay'd;
Far prouder of a brother's station there,
Than all the favours favour'd lovers boast.
"We quarrel'd once, and when I could no more

---

[4]The Larpent version has "Ere I had doubted this."

104

"The alter'd coldness of her eye endure,

"I slipp'd o' tip-toe to her chamber door;

"And when she ask'd who gently knock'd—Oh! oh!"

Who could have thought of this?

(*Throws himself into a chair, covers his face with his hand, and bursts into tears. After some time he starts up from his seat furiously.*)

Hell's direst torment seize th'infernal villain!

"Detested of my soul! I will have vengeance!

"I'll crush thy swelling pride—I'll still thy vaunting—

"I'll do a deed of blood—Why shrink I thus?"

If, by some spell or magick sympathy,

Piercing the lifeless figure on that wall[5]

Could pierce his bosom too, would I not cast it?[6] (*Throwing a dagger against the wall.*)

"Shall groans and blood affright me? No, I'll do it.

"Tho' gasping life beneath my pressure heav'd,

"And my soul shudder'd at the horrid brink,

"I would not flinch.—Fy, this recoiling nature!

"O that his sever'd limbs were strew'd in air,

"So as I saw him not!"

[5]The Larpent version has "Piercing that lifeless figure on the wall."
[6]The Larpent version has "thus would I cast it."

Don Juan

James Elroy Flecker
1910-11

Scene: Spain

Dramatic

Don Juan: a nobleman of Seville with an unsavory reputation, any age

Here, the legendary womanizer introduces himself and describes his life.

DON JUAN: I am Don Juan, curst from age to age
By priestly tract and sentimental stage.
Branded a villain or believed a fool,
Battered by hatred, seared by ridicule.
A lord on earth, all but a king in hell:
I am Don Juan with a tale to tell.
Hot leapt the dawn from deep Plutonian fires
And ran like blood among the twinkling spires.
The market quickened: carts came rattling down,
Good human music roared about the town.
And "come," they cried, "and buy the best of Spain's
Great fire-skinned fruits with cold and streaming veins."
Others: "The man who'd make lordly dish,
Would buy my speckled or my silver fish."
And some: "I stitch you raiment to the rule,"
And some: "I sell you attar of Stamboul,"
"And I have lapis for your love to wear,
Pearls for her neck, and amber for her hair."
Death has its gleam. They swing before me still,
The shapes and sounds and colours of Seville!
For there I learnt to love the plot, the fight,
The masker's cloak, the ladder set for flight,
The stern pursuit, the rapier's glint of death,
The scent of starlit roses, beauty's breath,
The music and the passion and the prize,
Aragon lips and Andalusian eyes.
This day a democrat I scoured the town;
Courting the next, I brought a princess down;

106

Now in some lady's panelled chamber hid
Achieved what love approves and law forbid;
Now walked and whistled round the sleepy farms
And clasped a Dulcinea in my arms.
I was the true, the grand idealist,
My light could pierce the pretty golden mist
That hides from common souls the starrier climes:—
I loved as small men do ten-thousand times:—
Rose to the blue triumphant, curved my bow,
Set high the mark and brought an angel low,
And laced with that brave body and shining soul
Learnt how to live, then learnt to love the whole.
And I first broke that jungle dark and dense
Which hides the silver house of Commonsense,
And dissipated that disastrous lie
Which makes a God of stuffless Unity,
And drave the dark behind me, and revealed
A pagan sunrise on a Christian field.
My legend tells that once by passion moved
I slew the father of a girl I loved:
Then summoned—like an old and hardened sinner—
The brand new statue of the dead to dinner.
My ribald guests with Spanish wine aflame
Were most delighted when the statue came,
Bowed to the party, made a little speech
And bore me off beyond their human reach.
Well, priests must flourish and the truth must pale:
A very pious entertaining tale.
But this believe. I struck a ringing blow
At sour authority's ancestral show,
And stirred the sawdust understuffing all
The sceptred or the surpliced ritual.
I will my happiness, kept bright and brave
My thoughts and deeds this side the accursed grave.
Life was a ten course banquet after all,
And neatly finished by my funeral.
"Pale guest, why strip the roses from your brow?

"We hope to feast till morning." Who knocks now?
"Twelve of the clock, Don Juan." In came he
That shining tall and cold authority
Whose marble lips smile down on lips that pray,
And took my hand, and I was led away.

The Great Divide

William Vaughn Moody
1906

Scene: a village in Massachusetts

Dramatic

Ghent: a man fighting for the woman he loves, 30s

Ghent saved Ruth from a group of toughs in a frontier town by purchasing her from them. A simple man, Ghent assumed that she was therefore his to keep. Some nine months later, they have a child. Ruth is finally able to make her way back home to Massachusetts, where she lives in shame with her family. Ghent has followed, and here eloquently pleads his love for her and their child.

GHENT: It's been no failure. However it is, it's been our life, and in my heart I think it's been—all—right!

[RUTH: All right! Oh, how can you say that? (*She repeats the words with a touch of awe and wonder.*) All right!]

GHENT: Some of it has been wrong, but as a whole it has been right—right! I know that doesn't happen often, but it has happened to us, because— (*He stops, unable to find words for his idea.*) —because—because the first time our eyes met, they burned away all that was bad in our meeting, and left only the fact that we had met—pure good—pure joy—a fortune of it—for both of us. Yes, both of us! You'll see it yourself some day.

[RUTH: If you had only heard my cry to you, to wait, to cleanse yourself and me—by suffering and sacrifice—before we dared begin to live! But you wouldn't see the need!— Oh, if you could have felt for yourself what I felt for you! If you could have said, "The wages of sin is death!" and suffered the anguish of death, and risen again purified! But instead of that, what you had done fell off from you like any daily trifle.]

GHENT (*Steps impulsively nearer her, sweeping his hand to indicate the portraits on the walls*): Ruth, it's these fellows are fooling you! It's they who keep your head set on the wages of sin, and all that rubbish. What have we got to do with suffering and sacrifice? That may be the law for some, and I've tried hard to see it as our law, and thought I had succeeded. But I haven't! Our law is joy, and selfishness; the curve of your shoulder and the light on your hair as you sit there says that as plain as preaching. —Does it gall you the way we came together? You asked me that night what brought me, and I told you whiskey, and sun, and the devil. Well, I tell you now I'm thankful on my knees for all three! Does it rankle in your mind that I took you when I could get you, by main strength and fraud? I guess most good women are taken that way, if they only knew it. Don't you want to be paid for? I guess every wife is paid for in some good coin or other. And as for you, I've paid for you not only with a trumpery chain, but with the heart in my breast, do you hear? That's one thing you can't throw back at me—the man you've made of me, the life and the meaning of life you've showed me the way to! (*Ruth's face is hidden in her hands, her elbows on the table. He stands over her, flushed and waiting. Gradually the light fades from his face. When he speaks again, the ring of exultation which has been in his voice is replaced by sober intensity.*) If you can't see it my way, give me another chance to live it out in yours. (*He waits, but she does not speak or look up. He takes a package of letters and papers from his pocket, and runs them over, in deep reflection.*) During the six months I've been East—

[Ruth (*Looking up.*): Six months? Mother said a week!]

GHENT: Your sister-in-law's telegram was forwarded to me here. I let her think it brought me, but as a matter of fact, I came East in the next train after yours. It was rather a low-lived thing to do, I suppose, hanging about and bribing your servant for news— (*Ruth lets her head sink in her hands. He pauses and continues ruefully.*) I might have known how that would strike you! Well, it would have come out sooner or later.—That's not what I started to talk about.—You ask me to suffer for my wrong. Since you left me I *have* suffered—God knows! You ask me to make some sacrifice. Well—how would the mine do? Since I've been away they've as good as stolen it from me. I could get it back easy enough by fighting; but supposing I don't fight. Then we'll start all over again, just as we stand in our shoes, and make another fortune—for our boy.

(*Ruth utters a faint moan as her head sinks in her arms on the table. With trembling hands, Ghent caresses her hair lightly, and speaks between a laugh and a sob.*) Little mother! Little mother! What does the past matter, when we've got the future—and him?

(*Ruth does not move. He remains bending over her for some moments, then straightens up, with a gesture of stoic despair.*)

I know what you're saying there to yourself, and I guess you're right. Wrong is wrong, from the moment it happens till the crack of doom, and all the angels in heaven, working overtime, can't make it less of different by a hair. That seems to be the law. I've learned it hard, but I guess I've learned it. I've seen it written in mountain letters across the continent of this life.—Done is done, and lost is lost, and smashed to hell is smashed to hell. We fuss and potter and patch up. You might as well try to batter down the Rocky Mountains with a rabbit's heartbeat! (*He goes to the door, where he turns.*) You've fought hard for me, God bless you for it.— But it's been a losing game with you from the first!— You belong here, and I belong out yonder—beyond the Rockies, beyond—the Great Divide!

The Great Galeoto

Jose Echegaray
1881

Scene: Madrid

#1—Serio-Comic
   Ernest: a frustrated playwright, 30s

The agony of writer's block is here defined by Ernest as he struggles to find words to put down on paper.

ERNEST (*Seated at table and preparing to write.*): Nothing —impossible! It is striving with the impossible. The idea is there; my head is fevered with it; I feel it. At moments an inward light illuminates it, and I see it. I see it in its floating form, vaguely outlined, and suddenly a secret voice seems to animate it, and I hear sounds of sorrow, sonorous sighs, shouts of sardonic laughter . . . a whole world of passions alive and struggling. . . . They burst forth from me, extend around me, and the air is full of them. then, then I say to myself: "Now is the moment." I take up my pen, stare into space, listen attentively, restraining my very heart-beats, and bend over the paper. . . . Ah, the irony of impotency! The outlines become blurred, the vision fades, the cries and sighs faint away . . . and nothingness, nothingness encircles me . . . the monotony of empty space, of inert thought, of idle pen and lifeless paper that lacks the life of thought! Ah! How varied are the shapes of nothingness, and how, in its dark and silent way, it mocks creatures of my stamp! So many, many forms! Canvas without color, bits of marble without shape, confused noise of chaotic vibrations. But nothing more irritating, more insolent, meaner than this insolent pen of mine (*Throws it away.*), nothing worse than this white sheet of paper. Oh, if I cannot fill it, at least I may destroy it— vile accomplice of my ambition and my eternal humiliation. Thus, thus . . . smaller and still smaller. (*Tears up paper. Pauses.*) And then! How lucky that nobody saw me! For in truth such fury is absurd and unjust. No, I will not yield. I will think and think, until either I have conquered or am crushed. No, I will not give up. Let me see, let me see . . . if in that way—

> When a friend tries to persuade Ernest to give up his struggle, the playwright
> perseveres, and he finally finds the words he was searching for.

ERNEST: Let Don Julian say what he will, I won't abandon the undertaking. That would be signal cowardice. Never retreat—always forward. (*Rises and begins to walk about in an agitated way. Then approaches the balcony.*) Protect me, night. In thy blackness, rather than in the azure clearness of day, are outlined the luminous shapes of inspiration. Lift your roofs, you thousand houses of this great town, as well for a poet in dire necessity as for the devil on two sticks who so wantonly exposed you. Let me see the men and women enter your drawing-rooms and boudoirs in search of the night's rest after fevered pleasures abroad. Let my acute hearing catch the stray words of all those who inquired for me of Don Julian and Teodora. As the scattered rays of light, when gathered to a focus by a diaphanous crystal, strike flame, and darkness is forged by the crossed bars of shadow; as mountains are made from grains of earth, and seas from drops of water: so will I use your wasted words, your vague smiles, your eager glances, and build my play of all those thousand trivialities dispersed in cafés, at reunions, theaters, and spectacles, and that float now in the air. Let the modest crystal of my intelligence by the lens which will concentrate light and shadow, from which will spring the dramatic conflagration and the tragic explosion of the catastrophe. Already my play takes shape. It has even a title now, for there, under the lamp-shade, I see the immortal work of the immortal Florentine. It offers me in Italian what in good Spanish it would be risky and futile audacity either to write on paper or pronounce on the stage. Francesca and Paolo, assist me with the story of your loves! (*Sits down and prepares to write.*) The play . . . the play begins . . . First page—there, it's no longer white. It has a name. (*Writing.*) *The Great Galeoto.* (*Writes feverishly.*)

Hellas

Percy Bysshe Shelley
1821

Scene: Constantinople

Dramatic
 Satan

Here, the Lord of Darkness reviles Christ when both gather at Constantinople for the conversion of Mahmud.

SATAN: Be as all things beneath the empyrean
Mine! Art thou eyeless like old Destiny,
Thou mockery-king, crowned with a wreath of thorns?
Whose sceptre is a reed, the broken reed
Which pierces thee! whose throne a chair of scorn;
For seest thou not beneath this crystal floor
The innumerable worlds of golden light
Which are my empire, and the least of them
Which thou wouldst redeem from me?
Know'st thou not them my portion?
Or wouldst rekindle the strife?
Which our great Father then did arbitrate
When he assigned to his competing sons
Each his apportioned realm?
Thou Destiny,
Thou who art mailed in the omnipotence
Of Him who sends thee forth, whate'er thy task,
Speed, spare not to accomplish, and be mine
Thy trophies, whether Greece again become
The fountain in the desert whence the earth
Shall drink of freedom, which shall give it strength
To suffer, or a gulf of hollow death
To swallow all delight, all life, all hope.
Go, thou Vicegerent of my will, no less
Than of the Father's; but lest thou shouldst faint,
The wingèd hounds, Famine and Pestilence,
Shall wait on thee, the hundred-forkèd snake,

Insatiate Superstition, still shall
The earth behind thy steps, and War shall hover
Above, and Fraud shall gape below, and Change
Shall flit before thee on her dragon wings,
Convulsing and consuming, and I add
Three vials of the tears which demons weep
When virtuous spirits through the gate of Death
Pass triumphing over the thorns of life,
Sceptres and crowns, mitres and swords and snares,
Trampling in scorn, like Him and Socrates.
The first is Anarchy; when Power and Pleasure,
Glory and science and security,
On Freedom hang like fruit on the green tree,
Then pour it forth, and men shall gather ashes.
The second Tyranny—

Hernani

Victor Hugo, tr. by Mrs. Newton Crosland
1830

Scene: Spain, 1519

#1—Dramatic
  Hernani: a bandit, 20–30

Here, the passionate Hernani vows to revenge himself against the treacherous Don Carlos.

HERNANI: One of thy followers! I am, oh King!
Well said. For night and day and step by step
I follow thee, with eye upon thy path
And dagger in my hand. My race in me
Pursues thy race in thee. And now behold
Thou art my rival! For an instant I
'Twixt love and hate was balanced in the scale.
Not large enough my heart for her and thee;
In loving her oblivious I became
Of all my hate of thee. But since 'tis thou
That comes to will I should remember it,
I recollect. My love it is that tilts
Th' uncertain balance, while it falls entire
Upon the side of hate. Thy follower!
'Tis thou hast said it. Never courtier yet
Of thy accursed court, or noble, fain
To kiss thy shadow—not a seneschal
With human heart abjured in serving thee;
No dog within thy palace, trained the King
To follow, will thy steps more closely haunt
And certainly than I. What they would have,
These famed grandees, is hollow title, or
Some toy that shines—some golden sheep to hang
About the neck. Not such a fool am I.
What I would have is not some favour vain,
But 'tis thy blood, won by my conquering steel—
Thy soul from out thy body forced—with all

That at the bottom of thy heart was reached
After deep delving. Go—you are in front—
I follow thee. My watchful vengeance walks
With me, and whispers in mine ear. Go where
Thou wilt, I'm there to listen and to spy,
And noiselessly my step will press on thine.
No day, shouldst thou but turn thy head, oh King,
But thou wilt find me, motionless and grave,
At festivals; at night, should'st thou look back,
Still wilt thou see my flaming eyes behind.
(*Exit by the little door.*)

#2—Dramatic
 Don Ruy: a man in love with a younger woman, 50-60

 Even though he knows of her love for Hernani, Don Ruy is determined to marry
 the beautiful Dona Sol.

DON RUY (*Rising, and going towards her.*): Now list. One cannot be
The mast of himself, so much in love
As I am now with thee. And I am old
And jealous, and am cross—and why? Because
I'm old; because the beauty, grace, or youth
Of others frightens, threatens me. Because
While jealous thus of others, of myself
I am ashamed. What mockery! that this love
Which to the heart brings back such joy and warmth,
Should halt, and but rejuvenate the soul,
Forgetful of the body. When I see
A youthful peasant, singing blithe and gay,
In the green meadows, often then I muse—
I, in my dismal paths, and murmur low:
"Oh, I would give my battlemented towers,
And ancient ducal donjon, and my fields
Of corn, and all my forest lands, and flocks
So vast which feed upon my hills, my name
And all my ancient title—ruins mine,
And ancestors who must expect me soon,
All—all I'd give for his new cot, and brow

Unwrinkled. For his hair is raven black,
And his eyes shine like yours. Beholding him
You might exclaim: A young man this! And then
Would think of me so old." I know it well
I am named Silva. Ah, but that is not
Enough; I say it, see it. Now behold
To what excess I love thee. All I'd give
Could I be like thee—young and handsome now!
Vain dream! that I were young again, who must
By long, long years precede thee to the tomb.
[*DONA SOL:* Who knows?]
DON RUY: And yet, I pray you, me believe,
The frivolous swains have not so much of love
Within their hearts as on their tongues. A girl
May love and trust one; if she dies for him,
He laughs. The strong-winged and gay-painted birds
That warble sweet, and in the thicket trill,
Will change their loves as they their plumage moult;
They are the old, with voice and colour gone,
And beauty fled, who have the resting wings
We love the best. Our steps are slow, and dim
Our eyes. Our brows are furrowed,—but the heart
Is never wrinkled. When an old man loves
He should be spared. The heart is ever young,
And always it can bleed. This love of mine
Is not a plaything made of glass to shake
And break. It is a love severe and sure,
Solid, profound, paternal,—strong as is
The oak which forms my ducal chair. See then
How well I love thee—and in other ways
I love thee—hundred other ways, e'en as
We love the dawn, and flowers, and heaven's blue!
To see thee, mark thy graceful step each day,
Thy forehead pure, thy brightly beaming eye,
I'm joyous—feeling that my soul will have
Perpetual festival!

> Here, the infamous outlaw pleads with Dona Sol to forsake the love that they share.

HERNANI: Alas! I have
Blasphemed! If I were in thy place I should
Be weary of the furious madman, who
Can only pity after he has struck.
I'd bid him go. Drive me away, I say,
And I will bless thee, for thou hast been good
And sweet. Too long thou hast myself endured,
For I am evil; I should blacken still
Thy days with my dark nights. At last it is
Too much; thy soul is lofty, beautiful,
And pure; if I am evil, is't thy fault?
Marry the old duke then, for he is good
And noble. By the mother's side he has
Olmédo, by his father's Alcala.
With him be rich and happy by one act.
Know you not what this generous hand of mine
Can offer thee of splendour? Ah, alone
A dowry of misfortune, and the choice
Of blood or tears. Exile, captivity
And death, and terrors that environ me.
These are thy necklaces and jewelled crown.
Never elated bridegroom to his bride
Offered a casket filled more lavishly,
But 'tis with misery and mournfulness.
Marry the old man—he deserves thee well!
Ah, who could ever think my head proscribed
Fit mate for forehead pure? What looker-on
That saw thee calm and beautiful, me rash
And violent—thee peaceful, like a flower
Growing in shelter, me by tempests dash'd
On rocks unnumbered—who could dare to say
That the same law should guide our destinies?
No, God, who ruleth all things well, did not

Make thee for me. No right from Heav'n above
Have I to thee; and I'm resigned to fate.
I have thy heart; it is a theft! I now
Unto a worthier yield it. Never yet
Upon our love has Heaven smiled; 'tis false
If I have said thy destiny it was.
To vengeance and to love I bid adieu!
My life is ending; useless I will go,
And take away with me my double dream,
Ashamed I could not punish, nor could charm.
I have been made for hate, who only wished
To love. Forgive and fly me, these my prayers
Reject them not, since they will be my last.
Thou livest—I am dead. I see not why
Thou should'st immure thee in my tomb.

Joaquin Murieta de Castillo, The Celebrated California Bandit

Charles E. B. Howe

1858

Scene: a monastery in Mexico

#1—Dramatic
Joaquin: an orphaned youth raised in a monastery, 18

Brooding Joaquin has lived his entire life behind the protective walls of the monastery. Here, he muses on his strange and empty existence.

JOAQUIN: Oh, how gloomy these walls have become. They are hateful to my sight; for their darksome shadow finds a reflection in my thoughts, and makes me sick at heart. What is there to cure this despondency? What thought, of all I have read, will aid to dispel these fancies of a home and a mother? I never knew what it was to have maternal care; yet how precious is the very sound of such a name as mother; and when connected with the name of home, oh how much more dear it sounds! There's a charm in the words that thrills through me as if they were electricity. Mother and Home! From all that I have heard of them, I have learned to long for their existence; yet I know them only by name. The blessed of this world are those who have a mother to counsel with and guide them, and the roof-tree to shelter them in hours as dark as mine. Mother and Home! I never tire repeating them. Then again, in my dark visions I see a fairy form that lights up and adds the glory of loveliness to my musings. That could not be my mother, for I have watched the wild blast of the hurricane and trembled, and that same form would glide before me, and all seemed pleasant—even the dread havoc that the wild wind caused seemed less fearful in its destruction. I have watched the stars, until my eyes grew weary with grazing on their twinkling orbs, and this form has passed, and I have forgot myself in her invisible presence. I have walked amid the flowers, and their rich blossoms gave forth no perfume, until her image crossed my path, and then I bemoaned, because the humming bird intercepted their odor. What fairy can this be? Is there a reality for these wild fancies? Yes; it is possible there is some place in this world inhabited by my vision; then why not leave these walls and go forth into the world and seek her? But what do I know of the world or its people? for I have not seen much of its surface, or associated with them. Yet I wish I was free, to act, to do for myself. I will—yes, I will be free! I am a prisoner here. This night I will leave this cell, and forever! What words? I am surprised at the very thought, and more so at their utterance. But shall I endure this serfdom? tremble when the Superior comes, to show him that I am a peon—a slave? observe his humor, and play the puppet to conciliate his favor? Oh, I have crouched at his look as a sloth hound does under the lash of his master. And to continue thus for days, weeks, months to come; no! I would rather be transformed to a monkey, and play in freedom on the boughs of a tree, than submit to confinement within these walls another space marked by a day. I want freedom; yet I tremble at the uncertainty before me. But I will be free; and this night, though the venom of my dagger's sting pierces a body more precious than the Pope's. (*A noise without.*) Psst! What noise is that? Who should invade the secrecy of my cell at this hour of the night? I will extinguish the light and use my dark lantern for I fear, I know not what; for this is an untimely visit.

#2—Dramatic
 Garcia: a ruthless bandit and murderer, 30–50

 When his life is spared by young Joaquin, Garcia impulsively vows to never harm his savior. When Joaquin subsequently rescues a band of pioneers that Garcia had threatened to rob and kill, the bandit rages privately.

GARCIA: Joaquin has dared to interfere between the wolf and its victims. Hell's curse! That I should hold that oath so binding, when to cut his throat would release me from all promises. What is one life? Have I not taken twenty—aye, fifty—better, far better than his; and for less gold than old Gonzalles offered? To say I will kill Joaquin is easier said than done. I have seen him asleep close by my side, as unconscious as if he were in no danger; yet it seemed to me that whenever I approached him, with that thought on my mind, he would move uneasily in his sleep, and his eyes would open, as if his very eyes and ears did nothing but spy my acts and learn the fall of my footsteps. I hate him! No; I do not love him; then by hell and its furies, I fear him. A boy! caramba! I may just as well say I have found a master; Curse the name! I once had a master. Hell! how my blood boils! That master was my father; my mother his slave, and I born his peon. How I have seen that man whip my mother. Large scars showed their hideousness all over her once beautiful face. She said she was once beautiful—and I believe her. That master whipped my mother once too often. It was in a by-place; I heard the lash falling on the back of one begging for mercy; I hurried to the spot—it was my mother, bleeding at every blow; I felled the hound of hell to the earth—my master, my father—I plucked his eyes out; and then he begged for what he had refused to give, Mercy. I cut limb from limb of his body; his heart I trampled under my feet. I was blood—all I saw was blood. And then my mother embraced me and called me her child—(*Laughs*.)—and I became a fiend. When I think of that first act, I could drink blood. The Past—the awful Past—I cannot think of it! What a hell is conscience!

Judith

Friedrich Hebbel
1840

Scene: Bethulia

#1—Dramatic
> Holofernes: the Tyrant of Babylon; a violent and evil man, 40s

> Here, the dread general of Nebuchadnezzer muses on the importance of keeping himself a mystery to his underlings.

HOLOFERNES: (*Alone.*) That's the real art: not to let yourself be calculated, but always to stay a mystery. Water does not know this, so they've dammed the sea and dug a bed for the river. Fire hasn't mastered the art either; it's fallen so low that the kitchen boys have investigated its nature and now it has to boil cabbage for any rascal who wants it. Not even the sun knows it: they've spied out its path and shoemakers and tailors measure time by its shadows. But I have mastered the art! They lurk about me and peer into the cracks and crevices of my soul, and, out of every word I utter, they try to forge a wrench to open up the chambers of my heart. But my present is never consistent with my past; I am not one of those fools who fall flat on their faces in cowardly vanity and make each day the other's fool; no, I cheerfully hack up today's Holofernes into little pieces and feed him to tomorrow's Holofernes. I don't see merely a dull feeding process in life, but rather a steady transformation and rebirth of existence. Indeed, at times, I feel among all these fools that I am alone, as though they could only become aware of themselves if I cut off their arms and legs. They notice this more and more, but, instead of climbing up on top of me, they wretchedly withdraw from me and flee like a rabbit who flees from fire which might singe his whiskers. If I only had one enemy, just one, who'd dare to confront me! I'd kiss him; indeed, after I'd made him bite the dust, in hot battle, I'd throw myself upon him and die with him! Nebuchadnezzar is, unfortunately, nothing but an arrogant cipher who passes time by eternally multiplying himself. If I subtract myself and Assyria, nothing remains but a human skin stuffed with fat. I want to conquer the world for him, and, when he has it, I want to take it away from him!

The general finds himself attracted to Judith, a captured Jew who is secretly plotting to kill him. Here, the self-centered man contemplates his assured victory over Judith, while especially relishing the thought of driving the God she loves from her heart.

HOLOFERNES: Did you try her? (*Officer is embarrassed and silent. Holofernes, wild with anger.*) You dared to do that and knew that she pleases me? Take that, you dog! (*He strikes him down.*) Take him away, and bring the woman to me. It's a shame that she walks among us Assyrians untouched!— (*The body is taken away.*) A woman is a woman, and still, one imagines there is a difference. Of course, a man feel his worth more when embracing a woman than anywhere else. Ha! When, in conflict between their sensual pleasure and chastity, they tremble as they anticipate the man's embrace! When they look as though they wanted to flee, and then, suddenly overcome by their nature, they throw their arms around his neck, when their last bit of independence and self-assurance rises up and spurs them, unable to resist any longer, to cooperate willingly. If then their desire, aroused in every drop of their blood by treacherous kisses, begins to race against the man's, so that they invite where they should be resisting—yes, that is life—then one finds out why the gods took the trouble to create man; there's a satisfaction, an overflowing measure of it! And completely so, if their petty soul had been filled with hatred and cowardly anger just the moment before, if their eyes, now tearful with joy, had closed darkly when the conqueror entered, when the hand which now squeezes his fondly would have been glad to mix poison into his wine but a minute ago! That's a triumph unlike any other, and I've enjoyed it many times. This Judith too—to be sure, her eyes look kind, and her cheeks smile like sunshine; but no one but her God dwells in her heart, and I'd like to drive him out now. When I was a young man and encountered an enemy, I'd sometimes wrestle with him until I had his sword and would then slay him with it instead of drawing my own. That's how I'd like to slay her. She's to dissolve before me because of her own feeling, because of the faithlessness of her senses!

As he prepares to seduce Judith, Holofernes can not help taking a moment to preen in front of his captive.

HOLOFERNES (*To the valet.*): Prepare my bed! (*Valet off.*) Behold, woman, these arms of mine have been dipped in blood up to the elbows; every one of my thoughts spawns atrocities and destruction; my very word is death! The world seems pitiable to me! I feel that I was born to destroy it so that something better may take its place. They curse me, but their curse does not cling to my soul; it merely bats its wings and shakes it off as though it were nothing. So, I suppose, I'm justified. "Oh, Holofernes, you don't know how this feels!" a man groaned once who was being roasted alive in a red hot oven at my command. "I really don't," I said and lay down next to him. Don't admire me for that; it was foolish.

[JUDITH (*To herself.*): Stop! Stop! I'll have to kill him if I am not to kneel before him!]

HOLOFERNES: Strength! Strength is what it is! Let him come who can hurl me to the ground! I long for him! It is tedious to be able to honor nothing but oneself! Let him grind me in a mortar and, if it pleases him, fill in the hole I tore into the world with the hash he makes of me! I bore further and further with my sword. If the blood-curdling screams for help fail to rouse the savior, then none exists. The hurricane rushes through the world and looks for its brother. But it uproots the oaks which appear to defy him, topples the towers, and lifts the globe out of its joints. Only then does it realize that it has no equal and goes to sleep in disgust. I wonder whether Nebuchadnezzar is my brother. He's certainly my Lord. Perhaps, some day, he'll throw my head to the dogs; I hope this food will agree with them! Perhaps some day I'll feed his entrails to the tigers of Assyria. Then, yes, then I'll know that I am the measure of mankind, and, for an eternity, I'll stand before man's dizzied eyes as an unreachable god girded with horror! Oh that last moment, the last! I wish it had arrived! "Come, all of whom I have hurt!" I'll exclaim, "you, whom I've crippled, you, whose wives I tore from your embrace, whose daughters I've snatched from your side, come, think up tortures for me! Tap my blood and make me drink it; cut flesh from my loins and give it to me to eat!" And when they think they've done their worst to me, and I name something still worse, and ask them in a kindly manner not to deny me that; when they then stand about in terrified astonishment and I'm persuading them with a smile to death and madness, with a smile in spite of all my suffering, then I shall roar at them: "Kneel, for I am your god!" and I'll close my lips and eyes and shall die quietly and in secret.

The Lady of Lyons

Edward Bulwer-Lytton
1838

Scene: Alsace

Serio-Comic
   Melnotte: a young man in love, 20s

   Melnotte is a simple country boy who has fallen in love with the daughter of a
   wealthy merchant. When his mother chides him for courting a woman above his
   station, he assures her that he is more than capable of achieving his goal.

MELNOTTE: Do the stars think of us? Yet if the prisoner see them
shine into his dungeon, wouldst thou bid him turn away from *their*
lustre? Even so from this low cell, poverty, I lift my eyes to Pauline
and forget my chains.— (*Goes to the picture and draws aside the curtain.*)
See, this is her image—painted from memory. Oh, how the canvas
wrongs her!— (*Takes up the brush and throws it aside.*) I shall never be a
painter! I can paint no likeness but one, and that is above all art. I
would turn soldier—France needs soldiers! But to leave the air that
Pauline breathes! What is the hour?—so late? I will tell thee a secret,
mother. Thou knowest that for the last six weeks I have sent every
day the rarest flowers to Pauline?—she wears them. I have seen them
on her breast. Ah, and then the whole universe seemed filled with
odors! I have now grown more bold—I have poured my worship into
poetry—I have sent the verses to Pauline—I have signed them with
my own name. My messenger ought to be back by this time. I bade
him wait for the answer.
[*WIDOW:* And what answer do you expect, Claude?]
MELNOTTE: That which the Queen of Navarre sent to the poor trou-
badour:—"Let me see the Oracle that can tell nations I am beautiful!"
She will admit me. I shall hear her speak—I shall meet her eyes—I
shall read upon her cheek the swept thoughts that translate themselves into blushes. Then—then, oh, then—she may forget that I am
the peasant's son!
[*WIDOW:* Nay, if she will but hear thee talk, Claude?]
MELNOTTE: I foresee it all. She will tell me that desert is the true
rank. She will give me a badge—a flower—a glove! Oh rapture! I

shall join the armies of the republic—I shall rise—I shall win a name that beauty will not blush to hear. I shall return with the right to say to her—"See, how love does not level the proud, but raise the humble!" Oh, how my heart swells within me!—Oh, what glorious prophets of the future are youth and hope!

Lady Windermere's Fan

Oscar Wilde
1891

Scene: London

Dramatic

Lord Darlington: a cad, 20–30

Here, Lord Darlington does his best to seduce the virtuous Lady Windermere.

LORD DARLINGTON: Between men and women there is no friendship possible. There is passion, enmity, worship, love, but no friendship. I love you—

[LADY WINDERMERE: No, no! (*Rises.*)]

LORD DARLINGTON: Yes, I love you! You are more to me than anything in the whole world. What does your husband give you? Nothing. Whatever is in him he gives to this wretched woman, whom he has thrust into your society, into your home, to shame you before everyone. I offer you my life—

[LADY WINDERMERE: Lord Darlington!]

LORD DARLINGTON: My life—my whole life. Take it, and do with it what you will. . . . I love you—love you as I have never loved any living thing. From the moment I met you I loved you, loved you blindly, adoringly, madly! You did not know it then—you know it now! Leave this house to-night. I won't tell you that the world matters nothing, or the world's voice, or the voice of society. They matter a good deal. They matter far too much. But there are moments when one has to choose between living one's own life, fully, entirely, completely—or dragging out some false, shallow, degrading existence that the world in its hypocrisy demands. You have that moment now. Choose! Oh, my love, choose!

[LADY WINDERMERE (*Moving slowly away from him and looking at him with startled eyes*): I have not the courage.]

LORD DARLINGTON (*Following her.*): Yes; you have the courage. There may be six months of pain, of disgrace even, but when you no longer bear his name, when you bear mine, all will be well. Margaret, my love, my wife that shall be some day—yes, my wife! You know it! What are you now? This woman has the place that belongs by right to you. Oh, go—go out of this house, with head erect, with a smile upon your lips, with courage in your eyes. All London will know why you did it, and who will blame you? No one. If they do, what matter? Wrong? What is wrong? It's wrong for a man to abandon his wife for a shameless woman. It is wrong for a wife to remain with a man who so dishonours her. You said once you would make no compromise with things. Make none now. Be brave! Be yourself!

The League of Youth

Henrik Ibsen

1869

Scene: a market town in Norway

Dramatic

    Stensgård: an idealist, 20–30

  Stensgård, an idealistic young attorney, here reveals his political ambition.

STENSGÅRD: To build up? We have to tear down first.— Fieldbo, I had once a dream—or did I see it? No; it was a dream, but such a vivid one! I thought the Day of Judgment was come upon the world. I could see the whole curve of the hemisphere. There was no sun, only a livid stormlight. A tempest arose; it came rushing from the west and swept everything before it: first withered leaves, then men; but they kept on their feet all the time, and their garments clung fast to them, so that they seemed to be hurried along sitting. At first they looked like townspeople running after their hats in a wind; but when they came nearer they were emperors and kings; and it was their crowns and orbs they were chasing and catching at, and seemed always on the point of grasping, but never grasped. Oh, there were hundreds and hundreds of them, and none of them understood in the least what was happening; but many bewailed themselves, and asked: "Whence can it come, this terrible storm?" Then there came the answer: "One Voice spoke, and the storm is the echo of that one Voice."

[*FIELDBO:* When did you dream that?]

STENSGÅRD: Oh, I don't remember when; several years ago.

[*FIELDBO:* There were probably disturbances somewhere in Europe, and you had been reading the newspapers after a heavy supper.]

STENSGÅRD: The same shiver, the same thrill, that then ran down my back, I felt again to-night. Yes, I will give my whole soul utterance. I will be the Voice—

Leonce and Lena

George Buchner, tr. by Henry J. Schmidt
1836

Scene: the mythical kingdom of Popo

Serio-Comic

Prince Leonce: a foolish young man, 20s

Privilege and sloth have turned Leonce into nothing short of a fop. Here, he lazily contemplates his feelings for Rosetta.

LEONCE (*Alone.*): Love is a peculiar thing. You lie half-asleep in bed for a year, then one fine morning you wake up, drink a glass of water, get dressed, and run your hand across your forehead and come to your senses—and come to your senses.—My God, how many women does one need to sing up and down the scale of love? One woman is scarcely enough for a single note. Why is the mist above the earth a prism that breaks the white-hot ray of love into a rainbow?— (*He drinks.*) Which bottle contains the wine that will make me drunk today? Can't I even get that far anymore? It's as if I were sitting under a vacuum pump. The air so sharp and thin that I'm freezing, as if I were going ice skating in cotton pants.—Gentlemen, gentlemen, do you know what Caligula and Nero were? I know.—Come, Leonce, let's have a soliloquy, I'll listen. My life yawns at me like a large white sheet of paper that I have to fill, but I can't write a single letter. My head is an empty dance hall, a few withered roses and crumpled ribbons on the floor, broken violins in the corner, the last dancers have taken off their masks and look at each other with dead-tired eyes. I turn myself inside out twenty-four times a day, like a glove. Oh, I know myself, I know what I'll be thinking and dreaming in a quarter of an hour, in a week, in a year. God, what have I done that you make me recite my lesson so often like a schoolboy?—

Bravo, Leonce! Bravo! (*He applauds.*) It does me good to cheer for myself like this. Hey! Leonce! Leonce!

The Liars

Henry Arthur Jones
1897

Scene: London

Serio-Comic
   Sir Christopher: a clever and philosophical man, 50s

   When his friend, Ned, plans to run off with the very married Lady Jessica, Sir Christopher does his best to talk them both out of their foolish passion.

SIR CHRISTOPHER: One moment, Ned! (*Takes out his watch, looks ruefully at his packing, half aside.*) Good lord! when shall I get on with my packing? (*Puts watch in pocket, faces Falkner and Lady Jessica very resolutely.*) Now! I've nothing to say in the abstract against running away with another man's wife! There may be planets where it is not only the highest ideal morality, but where it has the further advantage of being a practical way of carrying on society. But it has this one fatal defect in our country to-day—it won't work! You know what we English are, Ned. We're not a bit better than our neighbours, but, thank God! we do pretend we are, and we do make it hot for anybody who disturbs that holy pretence. And take my word for it, my dear Lady Jessica, my dear Ned, it won't work. You know it's not an original experiment you're making. It has been tried before. Have you ever known it to be successful? Lady Jessica, think of the brave pioneers who have gone before you in this enterprise. They've all perished, and their bones whiten the anti-matrimonial shore. Think of them! Charley Gray and Lady Rideout—flitting shabbily about the Continent at cheap *table d'hôtes* and gambling clubs, rubbing shoulders with all the blackguards and *demimondaines* of Europe. Poor old Fitz and his beauty—moping down at Farnhurst, cut by the county, with no single occupation except to nag and rag each other to pieces from morning to night. Billy Dover and Polly Atchison—

[*LADY JESSICA (Indignant.):* Well!]

SIR CHRISTOPHER: —cut in for fresh partners in three weeks. That old idiot, Sir Bonham Dancer—paid five thousand pounds for damages for being saddled with the professional strong man's wife.

George Nuneham and Mrs. Sandys—George is conducting a tramcar in New York, and Mrs Sandys—Lady Jessica, you knew Mrs. Sandys, a delicate sweet little creature, I've met her at your receptions—she drank herself to death, and died in a hospital. (*Lady Jessica moves a little away from Falkner, who pursues her.*) Not encouraging, is it? Marriage may be disagreeable, it may be unprofitable, it may be ridiculous; but it isn't as bad as that! And do you think the experiment is going to be successful in *your* case? Not a bit of it! (*Falkner is going to speak.*) No, Ned, hear me out. (*Turns to Lady Jessica.*) First of all there will be the shabby scandal and dirty business of the divorce court. You won't like that. It isn't nice! You won't like it. After the divorce court, what is Ned to do with you. Take you to Africa? I do implore you, if you hope for any happiness in that state to which it is pleasing Falkner and Providence to call you, I do implore you, don't go out to Africa with him. You'd never stand the climate and the hardships, and you'd bore each other to death in a week. But if you don't go out to Africa, what are you to do? Stay in England, in society? Everybody will cut you. Take a place in the country? Think of poor old Fitz down at Farnhurst! Go abroad? Think of Charley Gray and Lady Rideout. Take any of the other dozen alternatives and find yourself stranded in some shady hole or corner, with the one solitary hope and ambition of somehow wriggling back into respectability. That's your side of it, Lady Jessica. As for Ned here, what is to become of him? (*Angry gesture from Falkner.*) Yes, Ned, I know you don't want to hear, but I'm going to finish. Turn away your head. This is for Lady Jessica. He's at the height of his career, with a great and honourable task in front of him. If you turn him aside you'll not only wreck and ruin your own life and reputation, but you'll wreck and ruin his. You won't! You won't! His interests, his duty, his honour all lie out there. If you care for him, don't keep him shuffling and malingering here. Send him out with me to finish his work like the good, splendid fellow he is. Set him free, Lady Jessica, and go back to your home. Your husband has been here. He's sorry for what is past, and he has promised to treat you more kindly in the future. He's waiting at home to take you out. You missed a very good dinner last night. Don't miss another to-night. I never saw a man in a better temper than your husband. Go to him, and do, once for all, have done with other folly. Do believe me, my dear Ned, my dear Lady Jessica, before it is too late, do believe me, it won't work, it won't work, it won't work!

Manfred

Lord Byron
@1815

Scene: the high Alps

#1—Dramatic
> Count Manfred: a man tortured by his past, any age

> On a dark night, Manfred climbs into the mountains in order to summon the spirits that he hopes will have the power to end his earthly suffering.

MANFRED: The lamp must be replenish'd, but even then
It will not burn so long as I must watch.
My slumbers—if I slumber—are not sleep,
But a continuance of enduring thought,
Which then I can resist not: in my heart
There is a vigil, and these eyes but close
To look within; and yet I live, and bear
The aspect and the form of breathing men.
But grief should be the instructor of the wise;
Sorrow is knowledge: they who know the most
Must mourn the deepest o'er the fatal truth,
The Tree of Knowledge is not that of Life.
Philosophy and science, and the springs
of wonder, and the wisdom of the world,
A power to make these subject to itself—
But they avail not: I have done men good,
And I have met with good even among men—
But this avail'd not: I have had my foes,
And none have baffled, many fallen before me—
But this avail'd not:—Good, or evil, life,
Powers, passions, all I see in other beings,
Have been to me as rain unto the sands,
Since that all-nameless hour. I have no dread,
And feel the curse to have no natural fear,
Nor fluttering throb, that beats with hopes or wishes,
Or lurking love of something on the earth.
Now to my task.—

Mysterious Agency!
Ye spirits of the unbounded Universe,
Whom I have sought in darkness and in light!
Ye, who do compass earth about, and dwell
In subtler essence! ye, to whom the tops
Of mountains inaccessible are haunts,
And earth's and ocean's caves familiar things—
I call upon ye by the written charm
Which gives me power upon you—Rise! appear! (*A pause.*)
They come not yet.—Now by the voice of him
Who is first among you; by this sign,
Which makes you tremble; by the claims of him
Who is undying,—Rise! appear!—Appear! (*A pause.*)
If it be so.—Spirits of earth and air,
Ye shall not thus elude me: by a power,
Deeper than all yet urged, a tyrant-spell,
Which had its birthplace in a star condemn'd,
The burning wreck of a demolish'd world,
A wandering hell in the eternal space;
By the strong curse which is upon my soul,
The thought which is within me and around me,
I do compel ye to my will. Appear!

#2—Dramatic
    Count Manfred

> Manfred has caused the death of the woman he loved and now his soul is also
> dead. Here, he looks upon the beauty of the Earth but is unmoved by it.

MANFRED: The spirits I have raised abandon me,
The spells which I have studied baffle me,
The remedy I reck'd of tortured me;
I lean no more on super-human aid,
It hath no power upon the past, and for
The future, till the past be gulf'd in darkness,
It is not of my search.—My mother Earth!
And thou fresh breaking Day, and you, ye Mountains,
Why are ye beautiful? I cannot love ye.
And thou, the bright eye of the universe,

That openest over all, and unto all
Art a delight—thou shin'st not on my heart.
And you, ye crags, upon whose extreme edge
I stand, and on the torrent's brink beneath
Behold the tall pines dwindled as to shrubs
In dizziness of distance; when a leap,
A stir, a motion, even a breath, would bring
My breast upon its rocky bosom's bed
To rest for ever—wherefore do I pause?
I feel the impulse—yet I do not plunge;
I see the peril—yet do not recede;
And my brain reels—and yet my foot is firm.
There is a power upon me which withholds,
And makes it my fatality to live;
If it be life to wear within myself
This barrenness of spirit, and to be
My own soul's sepulchre, for I have ceased
To justify my deeds unto myself—
The last infirmity of evil. Ay,
Thou winged and cloud-cleaving minister,
(An eagle passes.)
Whose happy flight is highest into heaven,
Well may'st thou swoop so near me—I should be
Thy prey, and gorge thine eaglets; thou art gone
Where the eye cannot follow thee; but thine
Yet pierces downward, onward, or above,
With a pervading vision.—Beautiful!
How beautiful is all this visible world!
How glorious in its action and itself!
But we, who name ourselves its sovereigns, we,
Half dust, half deity, alike unfit
To sink or soar, with our mix'd essence make
A conflict of its elements, and breathe
The breath of degradation and of pride,
Contending with low wants and lofty will,
Till our mortality predominates,
And men are—what they name not to themselves,

And trust not to each other. Hark! the note,
(*The Shepherd's pipe in the distance is heard.*)
The natural music of the mountain reed
(For here the patriarchal days are not
A pastoral fable) pipes in the liberal air,
Mix'd with the sweet bells of the sauntering herd;
My soul would drink those echoes.—Oh, that I were
The viewless spirit of a lovely sound,
A living voice, a breathing harmony,
A bodiless enjoyment—born and dying
With the blest tone which made me!

#3—Dramatic
    Count Manfred

> The ghost of Manfred's beloved has appeared to tell him that his time on Earth is
> at an end. Here, he observes his final sunset.

MANFRED: Glorious Orb! the idol
Of early nature, and the vigorous race
Of undiseased mankind, the giant sons
Of the embrace of angels with a sex
More beautiful than they, which did draw down
The erring spirits who can ne'er return;—
Most glorious orb! that wert a worship, ere
The mystery of thy making was reveal'd!
Thou earliest minister of the Almighty,
Which gladden'd, on their mountain tops, the hearts
Of the Chaldean shepherds, till they pour'd
Themselves in orisons! Thou material God!
And representative of the Unknown,
Who chose thee for his shadow! Thou chief star!
Centre of many stars! which mak'st our earth
Endurable, and temperest the hues
And hearts of all who walk within thy rays!
Sire of the seasons! Monarch of the climes,
And those who dwell in them! for near or far,
Our inborn spirits have a tint of thee,
Even as our outward aspects;—thou dost rise,

And shine, and set in glory. Fare thee well!
I ne'er shall see thee more. As my first glance
Of love and wonder was for thee, then take
My latest look: thou wilt not beam on one
To whom the gifts of life and warmth have been
Of a more fatal nature. He is gone;
I follow.

Marion de Lorme

Victor Hugo, tr. by George Burnham Ives
1831

Scene: France, 1638

Dramatic
> Didier: a man in love, 20s

Here, the impetuous Didier declares his passion for Marion.

DIDIER: Listen, Marie,
My name is Didier—no more. I never knew
Father or mother. In my infancy,
All naked I was left at a church door.
A woman, old and of the common people,
Having some spark of pity in her heart,
Took me with her, was nurse and mother to me;
She reared me as a Christian child, and then
She died and left me all her little store,
Nine hundred livres a year, on which I live.
Alone at twenty, life was sad and drear;
I travelled, saw mankind, and for some men
Conceived a bitter hatred, for the rest
Nought but contempt; for nowhere did I see
Aught else than pride, and want, and suffering,
Upon that tarnished mirror called the human face.
So here am I, still young, and yet in heart
Aged and weary of the world, as one might be
On going hence; nothing I touch that I
Wound not myself; evil the world appears,
But mankind worse.—Thus was I living on,
Poor, gloomy, and alone, when you appeared,
And brought me sweetest consolation.
I knew you not. In Paris 'twas, one night,
At a street corner, that I saw you first.
And afterward I met you now and then;
Your eyes were ever soft, and soft your speech.
I feared to love you, and I fled. Strange chance!

I find you here, I find you everywhere,
Even as my guardian angel. And at last,
Frantic with love, doubting, irresolute,
I dared to speak and you forbade me not.
Henceforth my heart and life are yours to rule.
What wish can I aid you to gratify?
What man or thing is troublesome to you?
Or is there aught that you would have, and is
There need that to obtain that thing for you,
Some one must die? must die without a word,
And deem his blood too well paid with a smile?
Is there such need? Command—for here am I.
[MARION (Smiling.): You are a strange man, but I love you so.]
DIDIER: You love me! Ah! beware! such words as those
Should not be said, alas! in thoughtless mood.
You love me? Do you know what true love is?
A love which doth become our blood, our light;
Which, if long held in check, takes fire, its flame
Burning still hotter, purifies the soul;
And which, alone in the heart's lowest depths,
Where we have heaped them up, consumes in its
Fierce blaze the debris of all passions else!
A love hopeless alike and limitless,
That, e'en returned, is sad and full of gloom!
—Tell me, is this the love you spoke of?
[MARION (Deeply moved.): Truly—]
DIDIER: Ah! you know not how ardently I love!
From the blest day I saw you first, my life,
Though sombre still, took on a brighter hue;
Your glances filled my darkness full of light.
Thenceforth all things were changed, and in my eyes
You shone refulgent, like a being from
An unknown world, of kindred with the angels.
This life, which my rebellious heart had spent
In lamentation, suddenly I saw
In a new light which made it almost fair;
For till the day you burst upon my sight,

Alone, an outcast, and oppressed, my days
Were passed in struggles and in misery.
I had not loved.

The Mollusc

Hubert Henry Davies
1907

Scene: London

Serio-Comic

Tom: a young man possessed of keen insight into life, 20-30

Tom is a member of an eccentric family, which he claims resembles molluscs.
Here, he defines his odd zoological thesis.

TOM: She's a mollusc.

[*MR. BAXTER:* What's that?]

TOM: Mollusca, subdivision of the animal kingdom.

[*MR. BAXTER:* I know that.]

TOM: People who are like a mollusc of the sea, which clings to a rock
and lets the tide flow over its head. People instead of moving, in
whom the instinct for what I call molluscry is as dominating as an inborn vice. And it is so catching. Why, one mollusc will infect a whole
household. We all had it at home. Mother was quite a famous mollusc in her time. She was bedridden for fifteen years, and then, don't
you remember, got up to Dulcie's wedding, to the amazement of
everybody, and tripped down the aisle as lively as a kitten, and then
went to bed again till she heard of something else she wanted to go
to—a garden party or something. Father, he was a mollusc, too; he
called it being a conservative; he might just as well have stayed in
bed, too. Ada, Charlie, Emmeline, all of them were more or less mol-
lusky, but Dulcibella was the queen. You won't often see such a fine
healthy specimen of a mollusc as Dulcie. I'm a born mollusc.

[*MR. BAXTER (Surprised.):* You?]

TOM: Yes, I'm energetic now, but only artificially energetic. I have to
be on to myself all the time; make myself do things. That's why I
chose the vigorous West, and wandered from camp to camp. I made
a pile in Leadville. I gambled it all away. I made another in Cripple
Creek. I gave it away to the poor. If I made another, I should chuck it
away. Don't you see why? Give me a competence, nothing to work
for, nothing to worry about from day to day—why, I should become
as famous a mollusc as dear old mother was.

[*MR. BAXTER:* Is molluscry the same as laziness?]

TOM: No, not altogether. The lazy flow with the tide. The mollusc uses forces to resist pressure. It's amazing the amount of force a mollusc will use, to do nothing, when it would be so much easier to do something. It's no fool, you know, it's often the most artful creature, it wriggles and squirms, and even fights from the instinct not to advance. There are wonderful things about molluscry, things to make you shout with laughter, but it's sad enough, too—it can ruin a life so, not only the life of the mollusc, but all the lives in the house where it dwells.

[*MR. BAXTER:* Is there no cure for molluscry?]

TOM: Well, I should say once a mollusc always a mollusc. But it's like drink, or any other vice. If grappled with it can be kept under. If left to itself, it becomes incurable.

Money

Edward Bulwer-Lytton
1840

Scene: London

Serio-Comic
  Graves: a recent widower, 30–40

  Here, a man of caustic sensibilities expresses his dislike of newspapers.

GRAVES: Ay—read the newspapers!—They'll tell you what this world is made of. Daily calendars of roguery and woe! Here, advertisements from quacks, money-lenders, cheap warehouses, and spotted boys with two heads! So much for dupes and impostors! Turn to the other column—police reports, bankruptcies, swindling, forgery, and a biographical sketch of the snub-nosed man who murdered his own three little cherubs at Pentonville. Do you fancy these but exceptions to the *general* virtue and health of the nation?—Turn to the leading article! and your hair will stand on end at the horrible wickedness or melancholy idiotism of that half of the population who think differently from yourself. In my day I have seen already eighteen crises, six annihilations of agriculture and commerce, four overthrows of the Church, and three last, final, awful, and irremediable destructions of the entire Constitution! And that's a newspaper—a newspaper—a newspaper!

The Octoroon

Dion Boucicault
1859

Scene: Terrebonne Plantation, Louisiana

Dramatic

      McClusky: an evil slave-owner, 30s

> To possess the beautiful Zoe, McClusky murders the mail carrier who was bring-
> ing evidence of her status as a freed slave. When his crime is discovered, he es-
> capes into the bayou where he is pursued by justice and nightmares.

MCCLUSKY: Burn, burn! blaze away! How the flames crack. I'm not
guilty; would ye murder me? Cut, cut the rope—I choke—choke! Ah!
(*Wakes.*) Hello! where am I? Why, I was dreaming—curse it! I can
never sleep now without dreaming. Hush! I thought I heard the
sound of a paddle in the water. All night, as I fled through the cane-
brake, I heard footsteps behind me. I lost them in the cedar swamp—
again they haunted my path down the bayou, moving as I moved,
resting when I rested—hush! there again!—no; it was only the wind
over the canes. The sun is rising. I must launch my dug-out, and put
for the bay, and in a few hours I shall be safe from pursuit on board
of one of the coasting schooners that run from Galveston to
Matagorda. In a little time this darned business will blow over, and I
can show again. Hark! there's that noise again! If it was the ghost of
that murdered boy haunting me! Well—I didn't mean to kill him, did
I? Well, then, what has my all-cowardly heart got to skeer me so for?

Otho the Great

John Keats
1819

Scene: Germany

Dramatic
    Albert: a German knight, 20s

    Albert has discovered the Lady Auranthe's treachery against the Emperor. As he
    returns to court, he mourns the passing of his youth and regrets his unwitting in-
    volvement in the traitorous plot.

ALBERT: O that the earth were empty, as when Cain
Had no perplexity to hide his head!
Or that the sword of some brave enemy
Had put a sudden stop to my hot breath,
And hurl'd me down the illimitable gulf
Of times past, unremember'd! Better so
Than thus fast-limed in a cursed snare,
The white limbs of a wanton. This the end
Of an aspiring life! My boyhood past
In feud with wolves and bears, when no eye saw
The solitary warfare, fought for love
Of honour 'mid the growling wilderness.
My sturdier youth, maturing to the sword,
Won by the syren-trumpets, and the ring
Of shields upon the pavement, when bright mail'd
Henry the Fowler pass'd the streets of Prague.
Was't to this end I louted and became
The menial of Mars, and held a spear
Sway'd by command, as corn is by the wind?
Is it for this, I now a lifted up
By Europe's throned Emperor, to see
My honour be my executioner,—
My love of fame, my prided honesty
Put to the torture for confessional?
Then damn'd crime of blurting to the world
A woman's secret!—Though a fiend she be,

Too tender of my ignominious life;
But then to wrong the generous Emperor
In such a searching point, were to give up
My soul for foot-ball at Hell's holiday!
I must confess, —and cut my throat,—to-day?
To-morrow? Ho! some wine!

Peer Gynt

Henrik Ibsen, tr. by Paul Green
1867

Scene: Norway

#1—Serio-Comic
Peer Gynt: a boastful and irresponsible young man, 20s

Here, the lazy Peer Gynt lies in a field watching the clouds go by and fantasizing that he is a great king.

PEER (*Almost snarling.*): Talk—Talk! Bite with your sharp tongues! Who cares! (*He lays himself back again, his hands under his head, staring up into the sky. The pain and sultry grief pass out of his face. His voice rises in a monologue, growing in fervency. The scene begins to fill again with the feeling of his mood—shadowing off into a darkening around him, but with a radiance filling the unseen sky above and silvering down on his face.*) I bet it's a million miles to that sky. Far, far. And there's a cloud up there, a teeny cloud and the wind blows it closer. It's got a shape to it— um—like a horse. (*His voice intense.*) And it's saddled and bridled, and a man riding. And behind an old woman on a broomstick. (*He laughs softly to himself.*) That's Mother. She running after me, quar- relling and screaming. (*Calling in a high, faraway voice.*) "You filthy pig! Hey there, Peer, Peer!" (*He is silent. His words are heard echoing across the valley, mocking and diminishing. For a moment he lies listening.*) Let her scream. For that's me riding on that horse, me riding there. Peer Gynt, and a multitude of folks are riding behind. That's my ser- vants. And look at my horse with its silver mane all r'ared up and his four gold horseshoes gleaming. Yay-ee, we go galloping in the sun! (*Excitedly.*) Like a great king riding in the sky! (*He sits sharply up.*) Peer Gynt on the highway of heaven. (*Staring up and off.*) And look there at the people waiting—a nation of people waiting. It's the Crown Prince of England, the beautiful women of England. (*Loudly.*) Greetings, sir. And for you lovely ladies jewels and a kiss for each pair of ruby red lips. (*Solveig and her father, a grave Lutheran minister, come in along the road on their way to the wedding. With them walks Aslak, the blacksmith, his tall form looming behind them. Solveig is a demure and beautiful young girl. Her hair hangs down her back like a cascade of gold, and she carries a white prayer book in her hand. Peer continues his mono-logue.*) They bow low before me. The King of England himself steps down from his throne to greet me. "King Peer," he says—

#2—Serio-Comic
    Peer Gynt

> Marooned in Morocco, Peer wanders the hot desert with his tattered umbrella and tries to make the best of his situation.

PEER (*Looking out toward the east and grimacing.*): Another wonderful day. The air smells like fresh manure, and the beetle is already up rolling his ball of dung in the dust. (*Peering off.*) And the morning, as the saying is, has gold in its mouth. (*He turns in toward the rocks at the right and stops. He staggers a bit from weakness and puts out his hand to steady himself.*) The city man talks of getting away from it all. He should come here. He could enjoy the silence of the country. (*He comes over near where the jewels and clothes are hidden. He gazes at the rock, which is now bathed in the golden light of the rising sun.*) So still you can hear yourself think. (*He scratches along the rocks hunting for something to eat. He puts on his pince nez with a foppish gesture and peers about him.*) Aha—a petrified toad, looking at the world and seeing nothing. (*Chuckling.*) Just being himself. (*He digs up an edible root and chews on it, then contemplates the stem.*) I've had meals that tasted better in my time. They say a man must humble himself before he shall be exalted. (*Chuckling again.*) I'm humble enough all right. (*He pulls up another root, chews on it and looks out over the desert.*) I wonder what God intends to do with all this sand. With proper machinery, a man might cut a canal, let the water in from the ocean. Soon this whole white-hot grave would grow green. Dew would drop from the sky and the people would build cities. And factories would be built. (*Firing up to his imagining.*) I could transplant the whole Norwegian race here from their cold climate. I could build a capital and call it Peeropolis. And the country would be name Gyntianna. (*Excitedly.*) Only money is needed to do it. Gold is the key. A new crusade against death! Gold—gold! (*In his growing fervor and excitement he pulls at a large plant growing in the rocks.*) Aye, I will send out the call of freedom over the world to bring the people to my kingdom. (*Echoingly.*) Kingdom? Half my kingdom for a horse! (*A horse whinnies close by at the right. He jumps back and in doing so jerks the plant up by the roots. A rock is dislodged and falls down. And there the great bundle of jewels spills open before him. He looks at them an instant incredulously and then glances up at the sky as if to acknowledge to whatever Power resides there that he, Peer Gynt, recognizes its beneficence. He salutes the sky with his hand.*) These gifts from heaven I acknowledge—a horse! and clothing! and jewels! (*The sky rumbles in jocose answer. Peer examines the jewels, fills his pockets, and then frenziedly begins putting on the rich coat and turban.*) They're the real thing. It's a miracle! They say faith can move mountains. But what about bringing a horse to pass in the middle of the desert? (*He reaches out his hand and clucks to the unseen horse. At this instant there sounds as if from a minaret in the sky the muezzin's call to morning prayer. Peer looks about him astounded. The call is repeated. The laughter of girls is heard tinkling in the air around him.*) And not only a horse, but girls. Jehovah improves.

#3—Dramatic
Peer Gynt

At the end of his life, Peer is confronted by visions of the countless things his vanity prohibited him from accomplishing. Here, Peer bemoans his wasted life just before he is transformed into a troll.

PEER: Leave me then. Fly on to your heaven! (*His shoulders shake with sudden sobs.*) Not even a reed to lean on—nothing but broken straws. (*He controls his sobs and wipes his eyes. Across the sky at the rear a falling star shoots with a streamer of flame. Peer looks at it and takes off his hat somewhat in awe and speaks gently and brokenly.*) Peer Gynt sends you greetings, Brother Falling Star. You have lighted your little hour and gone out in a yawn. (*He yawns and stands up a moment. Then he suddenly screams out in the silence.*) Is there nobody anywhere—nobody in the whole universe! No one in heaven or hell to help me! (*He falls down on his knees, his voice rising in an agony of half-sobbing soliloquy.*) Help me, help me! Somebody—where are you! But there is no one— no one. So poor can a soul become—so lonely when he goes back into nothingness, into the foggy emptiness. (*Kissing the ground.*) Oh, sweet and wonderful earth. Don't be angry with me, forgive me that I trampled your grass so uselessly with my heavy feet. (*He strokes the ground with his hands, then lifts his gnarled and weatherbeaten face.*) You sweet and glorious sun and wonderful earth, forgive me. You lighted my mother to no purpose, for I was conceived in the dark. And my birth was a penalty to be paid with my life. Let me go away, let me hide myself in the mountains. And there let the snow be piled high above me and a signboard on top with words that say, "Here lies nobody." And after that then—well, the rest is nothing.

Prometheus Unbound

Percy Bysshe Shelley
1820

Scene: a ravine of icy rocks in the Indian Caucasus

Dramatic

Prometheus: a man who dared to steal fire from the gods, 20–30

Prometheus has stolen from the gods and his punishment is to be nailed to a mountain where an eagle eats his liver by day, which then grows back by night. Here, the unhappy man curses the gods and his fate.

PROMETHEUS: Monarch of Gods and Dæmons, and all Spirits
But One, who throng those bright and rolling worlds
Which Thou and I alone of living things
Behold with sleepless eyes! regard this Earth
Made multitudinous with thy slaves, whom thou
Requitest for knee-worship, prayer, and praise,
And toil, and hecatombs of broken hearts,
With fear and self-contempt and barren hope;
Whilst me, who am thy foe, eyeless in hate,
Hast thou made reign and triumph, to thy scorn,
O'er mine own misery and thy vain revenge.
Three thousand years of sleep-unsheltered hours,
And moments aye divided by keen pangs
Till they seemed years, torture and solitude,
Scorn and despair—these are mine empire:
More glorious far than that which thou surveyest
From thine unenvied throne, O Mighty God!
Almighty, had I deigned to share the shame
Of thine ill tyranny, and hung not here
Nailed to this wall of eagle-baffling mountain,
Black, wintry, dead, unmeasured; without herb,
Inset, or beast, or shape or sound of life.
Ah me! alas, pain, pain ever, forever!
No change, no pause, no hope! Yet I endure.
I ask the Earth, have not the mountains felt?
I ask you Heaven, the all-beholding Sun,

Has it not seen? The Sea, in storm or calm,
Heaven's ever-changing shadow, spread below,
Have its deaf waves not heard my agony?
Ah me! alas, pain, pain ever, forever!
The crawling glaciers pierce me with the spears
Of their moon-freezing crystals; the bright chains
Eat with their burning cold into my bones.
Heaven's wingèd hound, polluting from thy lips
His beak in poison not his own, tears up
My heart; and shapeless sights come wandering by,
The ghastly people of the realm of dream,
Mocking me; and the Earthquake-fiends are charged
To wrench the rivets from my quivering wounds
When the rocks split and close again behind;
While from their loud abysses howling throng
The genii of the storm, urging the rage
Of whirlwind, and afflict me with keen hail.
And yet to me welcome is day and night,
Whether one breaks the hoar-frost of the morn,
Or starry, dim, and slow, the other climbs
The leaden-colored east; for then they lead
The wingless, crawling hours, one among whom—
As some dark Priest hales the reluctant victim—
Shall drag thee, cruel King, to kiss the blood
From these pale feet, which then might trample thee
If they disdained not such a prostrate slave.
Disdain! ah, no! I pity thee. What ruin
Will hunt thee undefended through the wide Heaven!
How will thy soul, cloven to its depth with terror,
Gape like a hell within! I speak in grief,
Not exultation, for I hate no more,
As then ere misery made me wise. The curse
Once breathed on thee I would recall. Ye Mountains,
Whose many-voiced Echoes, through the mist
Of cataracts, flung the thunder of that spell!
Ye icy Springs, stagnant with wrinkling frost,
Which vibrated to hear me, and then crept

Shuddering through India! Thou serenest Air
Through which the Sun walks burning without beams!
And ye swift Whirlwinds, who on poisèd wings
Hung mute and moveless o'er yon hushed abyss,
As thunder, louder than your own, made rock
The orbèd world! If then my words had power,
though I am changed so that aught evil wish
Is dead within; although no memory be
Of what is hate, let them not lose it now!
What was that curse? for ye all heard me speak.

Richelieu

Edward Bulwer-Lytton
1839

Scene: the court of King Louis XIII

#1—Serio-Comic
   The Chevalier de Mauprat: a young man in love, 20

This dashing young chevalier has fallen in love with Julie, the ward of the powerful Cardinal Richelieu. Here, de Mauprat gives voice to his passion.

DE MAUPRAT: Who, lonely in the midnight tent,

Gazed on the watch-fires in the sleepless air,

Nor chose one star amidst the clustering hosts

To bless it in the name of some fair face

Set in his spirit, as that star in Heaven?

For our divine affections, like the spheres,

Move over, ever musical.

[*BARADAS:* You speak

As one who fed on poetry.]

DE MAUPRAT: Why, man,

the thoughts of lovers stir with poetry

as leaves with summer-wind.—The heart that loves

Dwells in an Eden, hearing angel-lutes,

As Eve in the First

garden. Hast thou seen

My Julie, and not felt it henceforth dull

To live in the common world—and talk in words

That clothe the feelings of the frigid herd?

Upon the perfumed pillow of her lips—

As on his native bed of roses flushed

With Paphian skies—Love smiling sleeps:—Her voice

The blest interpreter of thoughts as pure

As virgin wells where Dian takes delight,

Or fairies dip their changelings!—In the maze

Of her harmonious beauties—Modesty

(Like some severer grace that lead the choir

Of her sweet sisters) every airy motion

Attunes to such chaste charm, that Passion holds
His burning breath, and will not with a sigh
Dissolve the spell that binds him!—Oh, those eyes
That woo the earth—shadowing more soul than lurks
Under the lids of Psyche!—Go!—thy lip
Curls at the purfled phrases of a lover—
Love thou, and if thy love be deep as mine,
Thou wilt not laugh at poets.
[BARADAS: (Aside.) With each word
Thou wak'st a jealous demon in my heart,
And my hand clutches at my hilt.—]
DE MAUPRAT: (Gayly.) No more!—
I love!—Your breast holds both my secrets!—Never
Unbury either!—Come, while yet we may,
We'll bask us in the noon of rosy life:—
Lounge through the gardens,—flaunt it in the taverns,—
Laugh,—game,—drink,—feast:—If so confined my days,
Faith, I'll inclose the knights.—Pshaw! not so grave;
I'm a true Frenchman!—*Vive la bagatelle!*

#2—Dramatic
    Cardinal Richelieu: the most powerful man in France, 40–50

    Richelieu takes a few moments in the dead of night to consider matters of life and death as well as his place in history.

RICHELIEU (Reading.):[7] "In silence, and at night, the Conscience
    feels
That life should soar to nobler ends than Power."
So sayest thou, sage and sober moralist!
But were thou tried? Sublime Philosophy,
Thou art the Patriarch's ladder, reaching heaven,

---

[7]The great length of this soliloquy adapts it only for the closet; but few of the lines are retained on the stage. To the reader, however, the passages omitted in representation will not, perhaps, be the most uninteresting in the play, and may be deemed necessary to the completion of the Cardinal's portrait—action on the stage supplying so subtly the place of words in the closet. The self-assured sophistries which, in the text, mingle with Richelieu's better-founded arguments, in apology for the darker traits of his character, are to be found scattered throughout the writings ascribed to him. The reader will observe that in this self-confession lies the latent poetical justice, which separates happiness from success.

And bright with beck'ning angels—but, alas!
We see thee, like the Patriarch, but in dreams,
By the first step—dull-slumbering on the earth.
I am not happy!—with the Titan's lust
I woo'd a goddess, and I clasp a cloud.
When I am dust, my name shall, like a star,
Shine through wan space, a glory—and a prophet
Whereby pale seers shall from their aëry towers
Con all the ominous signs, benign or evil,
That make the potent astrologue of kings.
But shall the Future judge me by the ends
That I have wrought—or by the dubious means
Through which the stream of my renown hath run
Into the many-voiced unfathom'd Time?
Foul in its bed lie weeds—and heaps of slime,
And with its waves—when sparkling in the sun,
Ofttimes the secret rivulets that swell
Its might of waters—blend the hues of blood.
Yet are my sins not those of *circumstance*,
That all-pervading atmosphere, wherein
Our spirits, like the unsteady lizard, take
The tints that color, and the food that nurtures?[8]
O! Ye, whose hour-glass shifts its tranquil sands
In the unvex'd silence of a student's cell;
Ye, whose untempted hearts have never toss'd
Upon the dark and stormy tides where life
Gives battle to the elements,—and man
Wrestles with man for some slight plank, whose weight
Will bear but one—while round the desperate wretch
The hungry billows roar—and the fierce Fate,
Like some huge monster, dim-seen through the surf,
Waits him who drops;—ye safe and formal men,
Who write the deeds, and with unfeverish hand
Weight in nice scales the motives of the Great,
Ye cannot know what ye have never tried!

....

[8]Retained in representation.

History preserves only the fleshless bones
Of what we are—and by the mocking skull
The would-be wise pretend to guess the features!
Without the roundness and the glow of life
How hideous is the skeleton! Without
The colorings and humanities that clothe
Our errors, the anatomists of schools
Can make our memory hideous!
I have wrought
Great uses out of evil tools—and they
In the time to come may bask beneath the light
Which I have stolen from the angry gods,
And warn their sons against the glorious theft,
Forgetful of the darkness which it broke.
I have shed blood—but I have had no foes
Save those the State had[9]—if my wrath was deadly,
'Tis that I felt my country in my veins,
And smote her sons as Brutus smote his own.[10]
And yet I am not happy—blanch'd and sear'd
Before my time—breathing an air of hate,
And seeing daggers in the eyes of men,
And wasting powers that shake the thrones of earth
In contest with the insects—bearding kings
And braved by lackeys[11]—murder at my bed;
And lone amidst the multitudinous web,

[9]It is well know that when, on his deathbed, Richelieu was asked if he forgave his enemies, he replied, "I never had any but those of the State." And this was true enough, for Richelieu and the State were one.
[10]Richelieu's vindication of himself from cruelty will be found in various parts of Petitot's Collection, vols. xxi.xxx (bis).
[11]Voltaire has a striking passage on the singular fate of Richelieu, recalled every hour from his gigantic schemes to frustrate some miserable cabal of the ante-room. Richelieu would often exclaim, that "Six pieds de terre," as he called the king's cabinet, "lue donnaient plus de peine que tout le reste de L'Europe." The death of Wallenstein, sacrificed by the Emperor Ferdinand, produced a most lively impression upon Richelieu. He found many traits of comparison between Ferdinand and Louis—Wallenstein and himself. In the Memoirs—now regarded by the best authorities as written by his sanction, and in great part by himself—the great Frenchman bursts (when alluding to Wallenstein's murder) into a touching and pathetic anathema on the misère de cete vie of dependence on jealous and timid royalty, which he himself, while he wrote, sustained. It is worthy of remark, that it was precisely at the period of Wallenstein's death that Richelieu obtained from the king an augmentation of his guard.

With the dread Three—that are the Fates who hold
The woof and shears—the Monk, the Spy, the Headsman.
And this is power? Alas! I am not happy.
(*After a pause.*)
And yet the Nile is fretted by the weeds
Its rising roots not up: but never yet
Did one least barrier by a ripple vex
My onward tide, unswept in sport away.
Am I so ruthless then that I do hate
Them who hate me? Tush, tush! I do not hate;
Nay, I forgive. The Statesman writes the doom,
But the Priest sends the blessing. I forgive them,
But I destroy; forgiveness is mine own,
Destruction is the State's! For private life,
Scripture the guide—for public, Machiavel.
Would fortune serve me if the Heaven were wroth!
For chance makes half my greatness. I was born
Beneath the aspect of a bright-eyed star,
And my triumphant adamant of soul
Is but the fixed persuasion of success.
Ah!—here!—that spasm!—again!—How Life and Death
Do wrestle for me momently? And yet
The king looks pale. I shall outlive the king!
And then, thou insolent Austrian—who didst gibe
At the ungainly, gaunt, and daring lover,[12]
Sleeking thy looks to silken Buckingham,—
Thou shalt—no matter!—I have outlived love.
O! beautiful—all golden—gentle youth!
Making thy palace in the careless front
And hopeful eye of man—ere yet the soul
Hath lost the memories which (so Plato dream'd)
Breathed glory from the earlier star it dwelt in—
Oh! for one gale from thine exulting morning,

---

[12]Richelieu was commonly supposed to have been too presuming in an interview with Anne of Austria (the queen), and to have bitterly resented the contempt she expressed for him. The Duke of Buckingham's frantic and Quixotic passion for the queen is well known.

Stirring amidst the roses, where of old
Love shook the dew-drops from his glancing hair!
Could I recall the past—or had not set
The prodigal treasures of the bankrupt soul
In one slight bark upon the shoreless sea;
The yoked steer, after his day of toil,
Forgets the goad, and rests,—to me alike
Or day or night—Ambition has no rest!
shall I resign?—who can resign himself?
For custom is ourself; as drink and food
Become our bone and flesh—the aliments
Nurturing our nobler part, the mind—thoughts, dreams,
Passions, and aims, in the revolving cycle
Of the great alchemy—at length are made
Our mind itself; and yet the sweets of leisure—
An honor'd home—far from these base intrigues—
An eyrie on the heaven-kiss'd heights of wisdom—
(*Taking up the book.*)
Speak to me, moralists!—I'll heed thy counsel.
Were it not best—

#3—Dramatic
   Richelieu

   During a disagreement, Louis XIII threatens to terminate Richelieu's power. The
   Cardinal here reacts with both fury and scorn.

RICHELIEU: Rivals, Sire, in what?
Service to France? *I have none!* Lives the man
Whom Europe, paled before your glory, deems
rival to Armand Richelieu?
[*LOUIS:* What, so haughty!
Remember, he who made, can unmake.]
RICHELIEU: Never!
Never! Your anger can recall your trust,
Annul my office, spoil me of my lands,
Rifle my coffers,—but my name—my deeds,
Are royal in a land beyond your sceptre!
Pass sentence on me, if you will; from kings,

Lo! I appeal to time! Be just, my liege—
I found your kingdom rent with heresies
And bristling with rebellion; lawless nobles
And breadless serfs; England fomenting discord;
Austria—her clutch on your dominion; Spain
Forging the prodigal gold of either Ind
To arm'd thunderbolts. The Arts lay dead,
Trade rotted in your marts, your Armies mutinous,
Your Treasury bankrupt. Would you now revoke
Your trust, so be it! and I leave you, sole
Supremest Monarch of the mightiest realm
From Ganges to the Icebergs:—Look without;
No foe not humbled!—Look within; the Arts
Quit for your schools—their old Hesperides
The golden Italy! while through the veins
Of your vast empire flows in strengthening tides
TRADE, the calm health of nations!
Sire, I know
Your smoother courtiers please you best—nor measure
Myself with them,—yet sometimes I would doubt
If Statesmen rock'd and dandled into power
Could leave such legacies to kings! (*Louis appears irresolute.*)
[*BARADAS: (Passing him whispers.*) But Julie,
Shall I not summon her to court?
*LOUIS (Motions to Baradas, and turns haughtily to the
Cardinal.*): Enough!
Your Eminence must excuse a longer audience.
To your own palace:—For our conference, this
Nor place—nor season.]
RICHELIEU: Good my liege, for *Justice*
All place a temple, and all season, summer!—
Do you deny me justice?—Saints of Heaven!
He turns from me!—*Do you deny me Justice?*
For fifteen years, while in these hands dwelt Empire,
The humblest craftsman—the obscurest vassal—
The very leper shrinking from the sun,
Though loathed by Charity, might ask for justice!—

Not with the fawning tone and crawling mien
Of some I see around you—Counts and Princes—
Kneeling for *favors;*—but, erect and loud,
As men who ask man's rights!—my liege, my Louis,
Do you refuse me justice—audience even—
In the pale presence of the baffled Murther?[13]

---

[13]For the haughty and rebuking tone which Richelieu assumed in his expostulations
with the king, see his *Memoirs* (*passim*) in *Petitot's Collection.*

The Rightful Heir

Edward Bulwer-Lytton
1868

Scene: England, 1588—the year of the Spanish Armada

Dramatic

Vyvyan: Captain of the *Dreadnought*, a privateer.

Vyvyan has just returned home from a long time at sea. During a joyful reunion with his wife, he takes a moment to correct her when she refers to the sea as being "cruel."

VYVYAN: She is not cruel if her breast swell high
Against the winds that thwart her loving aim
To link, by every raft whose course she speeds,
Man's common brotherhood from pole to pole;
Grant she hath danger—danger schools the brave,
And bravery leaves all cruel things to cowards.
Grant that she hardens us to fear,—the hearts
Most proof to fear are easiest moved to love,
As on the oak whose roots defy the storm
All the leaves tremble when the south-wind stirs.
Yet if the sea dismay thee, on the shores
Kissed by her waves, and far, as fairy isles
In poets' dreams, from this gray care-worn world,
Blooms many a bower for the Sea Rover's bride.
I know a land where feathering palm-trees shade
To delicate twilight, suns benign as those
Whose dawning gilded Eden;—Nature, there,
Like a gay spendthrift in his flush of youth,
Flings whole treasure on the lap of Time.
There, steeped in roseate hues, the lakelike sea
Heaves to an air whose breathing is ambrosia;
And, all the while, bright-winged and warbling birds,
Like happy souls released, melodious float
Thro' blissful light, and teach the ravished earth
How joy finds voice in Heaven. Come, rest we yonder,
And, side by side, forget that we are orphans.

Romance

Edward Sheldon
1913

Scene: a society party

Serio-Comic
  Van Tuyl: a man facing middle age, 51

When Van Tuyl discovers that the beautiful young Rita is attracted to him, he does his best to discourage her.

VAN TUYL: Rita, suppose we finish our—our friendship—end it here tonight.

[*RITA:* Tonight?—]

VAN TUYL: Give me your hand. There! Now we can talk!— I'm fond of you, dear—I always shall be that—but already I'm beginning to disappoint you. And I'm afraid I'll do it more and more as time goes on. (*Slight pause.*) Look at my hair! There wasn't any grey in it last year—at Millefleurs! But now—and next year there'll be more! And I've begun to be a little deaf and fall asleep in chairs and dream about tomorrow's dinner. My rheumatism, too, came back last week— (*She winces and draws away her hand.*) Don't blame me, dear—I can't help getting old.

[*RITA* (*Nervously.*): Don'—don' talk dat vay!]

VAN TUYL (*Quickly.*): God knows I'm not complaining! I've lived my life—and it's been very sweet. I've done some work, and done it pretty well, and then I've found time to enjoy a great many of the beautiful things that fill this beautiful world. (*Politely.*) Among them, my dear, I count your voice—and you! (*Resuming.*) And yet the fact remains I've lived my life, I'm in the twilight years—oh! they're golden yet, but that won't last, and they'll grow deep and dim until the last tinge of the sunset's gone and the stars are out and night comes—and it's time to sleep. (*With a change of tone.*) But you— Good Lord, *your* life has just begun! Why, the dew's still on the grass—it's sparkling brighter than your brightest diamonds! (*He touches the ornaments.*) The birds are singing madrigals, the meadow's burst into a sea of flowers—you wear the morning like a wreath upon your hair—don't lose all that, my dear—don't waste your springtime on a stupid fellow fifty-one years old!

Salomé

Oscar Wilde
1891

Scene: the court of Herod

Dramatic
>Herod, the Tetrarch of Judaea, 50s

>Here, lusty Herod begs his wife's daughter, Salomé, to dance for him.

HEROD: By my life, by my crown, by my gods. Whatsoever thou shalt desire I will give it thee, even to the half of my kingdom, if thou wilt but dance for me. O Salomé, Salomé, dance for me!

[*SALOMÉ:* You have sworn an oath, Tetrarch.]

HEROD: I have sworn an oath.

[*HERODIAS:* My daughter, do not dance.]

HEROD: Even to the half of my kingdom. Thou wilt be passing fair as a queen, Salomé, if it please thee to ask for half of my kingdom. Will she not be fair as a queen? Ah! It is cold here! There is an icy wind, and I hear . . . wherefore do I hear in the air this beating of wings? Ah! one might fancy a huge black bird that hovers over the terrace. Why can I not see it, this bird? The beat of its wings is terrible. The breath of the wind of its wings is terrible. It is a chill wind. Nay, but it is not cold, it is hot. I am choking. Pour water on my hands. Give me snow to eat. Loosen my mantle. Quick! quick! loosen my mantle. Nay, but leave it. It is my garland that hurts me, my garland of roses. The flowers are like fire. They have burned my forehead. (*He tears the wreath from his head and throws it on the table.*) Ah! I can breathe now. How red those petals are! They are like stains of blood on the cloth. That does not matter. It is not wise to find symbols in everything that one sees. It makes life too full of terrors. It were better to say that stains of blood are as lovely as rose petals. It were better far to say that. . . . But we will not speak of this. Now I am happy. I am passing happy. Have I not the right to be happy? Your daughter is going to dance for me. Wilt thou not dance for me, Salomé? Thou hast promised to dance for me.

[*HERODIAS:* I will not have her dance.

SALOMÉ: I will dance for you, Tetrarch.]

HEROD: You hear what your daughter says. she is going to dance for me. Thou doest well to dance for me, Salomé. And when thou hast danced for me, forget not to ask of me whatsoever thou hast a mind to ask. Whatsoever thou shalt desire I will give it thee, even to the half of my kingdom. I have sworn it, have I not?

[*SALOMÉ:* Thou hast sworn it, Tetrarch.]

HEROD: And I have never broken my word. I am not of those who break their oaths. I know not how to lie. I am the slave of my word, and my word is the word of a king. The King of Cappadocia had ever a lying tongue, but he is no true king. He is a coward. Also he owes me money that he will not repay. He has even insulted my ambassadors. He has spoken words that were wounding. But Caesar will crucify him when he comes to Rome. I know that Caesar will crucify him. And if he crucify him not, yet will he die, being eaten of worms. The prophet has prophesied it. Well! wherefore dost thou tarry, Salomé?

The Scarecrow

Percy MacKaye
1910

Scene: a village in Massachusetts, late 1600s

Dramatic
Ravensbane: a man bewitched, 20–30

The evil spirit of a scarecrow inhabits a mirror belonging to Ravensbane, and he
has fallen under its spell. Here, he addresses the figure in the mirror.

(*The same. Night. The moon, shining in broadly at the window, discovers
Ravensbane alone, prostrate before the mirror. Raised on one arm to a half-
sitting posture, he gazes fixedly at the vaguely seen image of the scarecrow
prostrate in the glass.*)

RAVENSBANE: All have left me—but not thou. Rachel has left me:
her eyes have turned away from me; she is gone. All that I loved, all
that loved me, have left me. A thousand ages—a thousand ages ago,
they went away; and thou and I have gazed upon each other's desert-
edness. Speak! and be pitiful! If thou art I, inscrutable image, if thou
dost feel these pangs thine own, show then self-mercy; speak! what
art thou? What am I? Why are we here? How comes it that we feel
and guess and suffer? Nay, though thou answer not these doubts, yet
mock them, mock them aloud, even as there, monstrous, thou coun-
terfeitest mine actions. Speak, abject enigma!—Speak, poor shadow,
thou—(*Recoiling wildly.*) Stand back, inanity! Thrust not they mawk-
ish face in pity toward me. Ape and idiot! Scarecrow!—to console
me! Haha!—A flail and broomstick! a cob, a gourd and pumpkin, to
fuse and sublimate themselves into a mage-philosopher, who dis-
courseth metaphysics to itself—itself, God! Dost Thou hear? Itself!
For even such am I—I whom Thou madest to love Rachel. Why,
God—haha! dost Thou dwell in this thing? Is it Thou that peerest
forth *at* me—*from* me? Why, hark then; Thou shalt listen, and answer—if Thou canst. Between the rise and setting of a sun, I have
walked in this world of Thine. I have been thrilled with wonder; I
have been calmed with knowledge; I have trembled with joy and
passion. Power, beauty, love have ravished me. Infinity itself, like a
dream, has blazed before me with the certitude of prophecy; and I

have cried, "This world, the heavens, time itself, are mine to conquer," and I have thrust forth mine arm to wear Thy shield forever—
and lo! for my shield Thou reachest me—a mirror, and whisperest:
"Know thyself! Thou art—a scarecrow: a tinkling clod, a rigmarole of
dust, a lump of ordure, contemptible, superfluous, inane!" Haha! Hahaha! And with such scarecrows Thou dost people a planet! O ludicrous! Monstrous! Ludicrous! At least, I thank Thee, God! at least this
breathing bathos can laugh at itself. Though hast vouchsafed to me,
Spirit,—hahaha!—to know myself. Mine, mine is the consummation
of man—even self-contempt! (*Pointing in the glass with an agony of de-
rision.*) Scarecrow! Scarecrow! Scarecrow!
[*THE IMAGE IN THE GLASS* (*More and more faintly.*): Scarecrow!
Scarecrow! Scarecrow!]
(*Ravensbane throws himself prone upon the floor, beneath the window, sob-
bing. There is a pause of silence, and the moon shines brighter.—Slowly
then Ravensbane, getting to his knees, looks out into the night.*)
RAVENSBANE: What face are you, high up through the twinkling
leaves? Do you not, like all the rest, turn aghast, your eyes away from
me—me, abject enormity, groveling at your feet? Gracious being, do
you not fear—despise me? O white peace of the world, beneath your
gaze the clouds glow silver, and the herded cattle, slumbering far
afield, crouch—beautiful. The slough shines lustrous as a bridal veil.
Beautiful face, you are Rachel's, and you have changed the world.
Nothing is mean, but you have made it miraculous; nothing is loathsome, nothing ludicrous, but you have converted it to loveliness, that
even this shadow of a mockery myself, cast by your light, gives me
the dear assurance I am a man. Rachel, mistress, mother, out of my
suffering you have brought forth my soul. I am saved!

The Tenor

Frank Wedekind, tr. by André Tridon
1899

Scene: a city in Austria

Dramatic
Gerardo: a Wagnerian tenor, 36

> When Gerardo is accosted in his hotel room by an obnoxious composer who believes that art is "... the highest thing in the world," the seasoned performer wastes no time in setting the young man straight.

GERARDO: Well, I despise the type of man that wastes his life in useless endeavor. What have you done in those fifty years of struggle, for yourself or for the world? Fifty years of useless struggle! That should convince the worst blockhead of the impracticability of his dreams. What have you done with your life? You have wasted it shamefully. If I had wasted my life as you have wasted yours—of course I am only speaking for myself—I don't think I should have the courage to look any one in the face.

[*DUHRING:* I am not doing it for myself; I am doing it for my art.]

GERARDO (*Scornfully.*): Art, my dear man! Let me tell you that art is quite different from what the papers tell us it is.

[*DUHRING:* To me it is the highest thing in the world.]

GERARDO: You may believe that, but nobody else does. We artists are merely a luxury for the use of the *bourgeoisie*. When I stand there on the stage I feel absolutely certain that not one solitary human being in the audience takes the slightest interest in what we, the artist, are doing. If they did, how could they listen to "Die Walküre," for instance? Why, it is an indecent story which could not be mentioned anywhere in polite society. And yet, when I sing Siegmund, the most puritanical mothers bring their fourteen-year-old daughters to hear me. This, you see, is the meaning of whatever you call art. This is what you sacrificed fifty years of your life to. Find out how many people came to hear me sing and many people came to gape at me as they would at the Emperor of China if he should turn up here to-morrow. Do you know what the artistic wants of the public consist in? To applaud, to send flowers, to have a subject for conversation, to see and be seen. They pay me half a million, but then I make business for hundreds of cabbies, writers, dressmakers, restaurant keepers. It keeps money circulating; it keeps blood running. It gets girls engaged, spinsters married, wives tempted, old cronies supplied with gossip; a woman loses her pocketbook in the crowd, a fellow becomes insane during the performance. Doctors, lawyers made. . . . (*He coughs.*) And with this I must sing Tristan in Brussels tomorrow night! I tell you all this, not out of vanity but to cure you of your delusions. The measure of a man's worth is the world's opinion of him, not the inner belief which one finally adopts after brooding over it for years. Don't imagine that you are a misunderstood genius. There are no misunderstood geniuses.

Uncle Vanya

Anton Chekhov, tr. by Stark Young
1899

Scene: a country estate in Russia

Dramatic

> Voinitsky (Uncle Vanya): a man who feels cheated by life, 47

Uncle Vanya has sacrificed his own dreams in order to run the country estate of his brother-in-law, whom all believe to be a great scholar. Uncle Vanya even gave up any claim he may at one time have had on the professor's wife, with whom he is still very much in love. When at last he discovers that the professor is a fake, he realizes that he has wasted his life and his love for nothing.

VOINITSKY (*Alone.*): She is gone— (*A pause.*)

Ten years ago I used to meet her at my dear sister's. She was seventeen then and I was thirty-seven years old. Why didn't I fall in love with her then and propose to her? It was so possible. And by now she would have been my wife—Yes—Now we both would have been awakened by the storm; she would have been frightened by the thunder and I would have held her in my arms and whispered: "Don't be afraid, I am here." Oh, beautiful thoughts, how wonderful, I am even smiling—but, my God, thoughts are getting tangled up in my head.—Why am I old? Why doesn't she understand me? Her speechifying, her lazy moralizing, her foolish, lazy thoughts about the end of the world—all that is hateful to me. (*A pause.*) Oh, how I was deceived! I adored that Professor, that pitiful, gouty creature, I worked for him like an ox! Sonia and I squeezed out of this estate its last drop of juice; like thrifty peasants we sold vegetable oil, beans, cottage cheese, went hungry ourselves so that out of pennies and half-pennies we might pile up thousands and send them to him. I used to be proud of him and his learning, I lived and breathed it! All he wrote and uttered seemed to me genius—God, and now here he is retired, and you can see now the whole sum of his life. After he is gone there won't be a single page of his work left behind; he is absolutely unknown, he is nothing! A soap bubble! And I've been fooled—I can see—stupid—fooled—